W9-BGC-501

STEVE GARFINK

RETIRE IN LUXURY
ON YOUR SOCIAL SECURITY

THE BEST CLAIMS STRATEGY FOR A
BETTER, LONGER, FREER RETIREMENT

International Living

Retire in Luxury on Your Social Security: The Best Claims Strategy
for a Better, Longer, Freer Retirement

Author: Steve Garfink

Editors: Sarah Condon and Laura Doyle

Cover photo: © Istockphoto.com/Christian Wheatley

ISBN: 978-1-911260-15-8   120B001037

© Copyright 2017. International Living Publishing Ltd., Woodlock House, Carrick Road, Portlaw, Co. Waterford, Ireland. All rights reserved. No part of this report may be reproduced by any means without the express written consent of the publisher. The information contained herein is obtained from sources believed to be reliable, but its accuracy cannot be guaranteed. Registered in Ireland No. 285214.

TABLE OF CONTENTS

Foreword.. 1

Introduction 5

Section I... 15

   Chapter 1: What "Everyone Knows" About Social Security—
Even if it's Wrong..18

   Chapter 2: From a Thread of Truth, a Tapestry of Baloney
and Mischief 26

   Chapter 3: Déjà Vu All Over Again: 1983—We Have Been
Here Before 34

   Chapter 4: How to Fix the Coming Social Security Shortfall..............51

   Chapter 5: Why Social Security Will be Fixed 71

   Chapter 6: Social Security: Part of the New Deal, Still a Good Deal....83

Section II 91

   Chapter 7: What Are Our Benefits Worth? 94

   Chapter 8: When to Start Benefits? Don't Look to the SSA for Help ... 101

   Chapter 9: Social Security Basics That May Apply to You 115

   Chapter 10: The Devil in the Dual Entitlement Details....................130

   Chapter 11: Just the Facts, Ma'am, Just the Facts............................141

Section III 153

   Chapter 12: Gaby Part I: A Single Woman Starts to Live
Her Dream..157

   Chapter 13: Gaby Part II: A Single Woman Starts to Live
Her Dream—Even Earlier 164

Chapter 14: Gaby Part III: Fixing a Broken Claiming Strategy 168

Chapter 15: Alison and Marcus: A Vacation Visit Leads to a
Change in Plans 175

Chapter 16: Simon and Michelle: She Wants to Volunteer
Closer to the Action 181

Chapter 17: Becky and Tony: Out of Financial Catastrophe to a
Brighter Future...187

Chapter 18: Sarah: Severe Claiming Pitfalls for Survivors 194

Chapter 19: Review, Conclusion, and Getting Started.....................199

Appendix A: Identifying the Key Pieces of Your Financial Puzzle...........208

Appendix B: *International Living* Resources 215

FOREWORD

Here's the good news: You can retire a lot sooner and a lot more comfortably than you may believe—if you're strategic in the way you manage your Social Security claim.

Most people are not. But this book will show you a path to claiming more...so you gain the flexibility and confidence to retire better—and maybe years earlier—than you ever thought you could.

Frankly, there's a lot of misinformation out there about Social Security. And the Social Security Administration itself will neither share the full story with you nor offer you advice.

You're on your own. And it's in this vacuum that you're at risk of missing out on opportunities to increase your Social Security benefit by tens—and even hundreds—of thousands of dollars.

By the time you've finished this book, however, you'll understand what the real situation is and how you can manage it to your advantage.

What you'll find, I think, is that you have many more options for a more comfortable, more engaging, and better-funded retirement than you may believe you have today.

As I said, most people leave their Social Security benefit to chance, assuming that by the time they're approaching retirement age, the die has been cast. In other words, most people think, "I guess I'll get what I get and it is what it is."

But that's not, in fact, the case.

You have way more control over the size of your Social Security benefit than you may realize.

Though most folks think about a Social Security benefit as a sort of "safety net" if you will…in fact, when handled the right way, your Social Security benefit is likely to be the single most valuable asset you have in retirement.

My point is: Most people underestimate its worth.

You can—and should—actively manage your claiming strategy when it comes to the Social Security benefit you'll receive. When you have a strong, well-thought-out strategy in place, you'll find you're in much more control of your retirement.

Not only will you likely have access to more income than you probably think you're due, but understanding how to manage your benefits effectively gives you the flexibility and freedom to retire not only better than you thought…but earlier, too. Two, five, even 10 years earlier than you may imagine.

When you layer in the incredible opportunities that exist today overseas to maximize your lifestyle and improve your quality of life while you spend less—you can see how a Social Security benefit really can fund a luxury retirement.

This book is designed to show, step-by-step, how it's done.

Section 1 addresses the debate around the viability of Social Security's funding. Lots of rhetoric gets tossed around about how Social Security is doomed. Not so, argues author Steve Garfink, and he makes a very compelling case as to why; this 2017 edition includes insights into the impact of the recent election on the overall prospects for the program. I believe, after reading this, that you will come away with a sense of confidence that Social Security will be there not just for you, but for your children and their children as well.

Section II unravels the complexities in the maze of rules governing how and when you can collect Social Security benefits. You'll find here lots of examples and scenarios that'll help you identify which rules are likely to apply to you at some point over the years. These become the touchstones you use when developing a personalized claiming strategy that will serve you best.

Section III helps you home in on that personalized claiming strategy. It walks you through the questions you need to consider and decisions you need to make so you can bring a measure of financial security to your retirement plans. In particular, Steve helps you consider these strategies in the context of an "International Living" lifestyle—that is, one that includes travel and good living with perhaps months, years, or even decades enjoyed overseas.

One of the many advantages of a Social Security benefit is that it can go wherever you go.

That's right. Anywhere in the world. You can arrange to have your payment deposited directly into a variety of correspondent banks in nearly every country around the world.

Or you can have your monthly benefit deposited—in the "regular way"—into your U.S. bank and manage the funds from there, much as you do with your other income. So if you're overseas, you can simply pull funds from an ATM, for instance.

The message—and the method—Steve Garfink shares here in these pages is straightforward, really. But it's remarkably powerful.

First, you have retirement options you probably don't realize you have—excellent options that will see you living better, retiring sooner, and enjoying life more.

Second, you have the power to maximize your Social Security benefits… but it's up to you to do it. In other words: You're well within your rights to create a strategy that makes good sense for you and your family, given your personal situation and your priorities. But you have to actively implement that strategy. The Social Security Administration won't do it for you. You've got to be your own advocate. Steve, in these pages, shows you how.

Third, if you like the idea of living rich... of enjoying a retirement that's stress-free, full of travel and adventure, and you thought that was the stuff of dreams...well, think again. It really IS possible to retire like a king on a Social Security payment.

And this book will show you exactly how...

Jackie Fl

Jackie Flynn
Publisher, *International Living*

INTRODUCTION

Consider two couples: Franny and Scott and Maria and Frank. They are all 62 years old, and if they start their Social Security benefits now, each couple can collect $2,300 a month. Each couple has found a retirement spot overseas where they can live on $2,000 a month, leaving about $300 a month ($3,600 a year), for trips home or to bring the grandchildren out for a visit. Sounds like a plan!

Both couples head off for their well-planned and long-dreamed-for retirement havens. After arriving and settling in at their respective destinations, both couples have $225,000 in savings to begin their adventure. (Both couples make conservative investments so their savings just keep up with inflation, after taxes. The numbers in this illustration are all in constant dollars; since Social Security is adjusted each year for inflation, the benefits more or less go up each year enough so you can buy the same amount of stuff over time as when you first started.)

They each settle in that first night at a cozy local restaurant and reflect on their good fortune. Life is good…

Different Claiming Strategies, Different Benefits

At age 85 our couples cross paths. (Although 85 may seem old to us, it is actually the average life expectancy for someone once they have reached age 62, according to the Social Security Administration's life expectancy calculator. Our two couples are about average in this regard.)

After fond greetings and reminiscences, they compare notes.

Franny: "Scott and I are so grateful for Social Security! We took our $2,300 a month in benefits when we turned 62, and it's still enough to basically cover all our living expenses. We haven't touched our nest egg one bit. It is very comforting to know we have $225,000 socked away for an emergency. We are so happy at how well it has all worked out. How have things gone for you guys?"

Maria and Frank exchange a nervous glance… "Well, it's worked out a bit differently for us," says Frank. "We followed a different claiming strategy, starting later, so our benefit is a bit over $4,000 a month, which is nice."

Scott: "Wow, you must have completely burned through your nest egg. Does that worry you?"

"Uh, not exactly," replies Maria. "Actually, we have about $340,000 in our nest egg now…"

"Wait," stammers Franny. "You collect $1,700 more a month in benefits than we do and you have $115,000 more in savings? How can that be?"

Why You Should Understand Claiming Strategy

How can that be, indeed? They are all exactly the same age, each started with identical potential benefits and savings, and both couples followed the same conservative investment strategy and the same monthly spending plan. They have reached their average life expectancy. Yet one couple collects 76% more per month in benefits and has 50% more money saved in the bank.

What's it like to learn at age 85 that you had other options, choices that would bring far greater wealth and income at a time of life when you are most vulnerable? Awkward! How would you feel if you were Franny and Scott?

The experiences of these couples illustrate the importance of claiming strategy in getting the most out of your Social Security benefits. Few baby boomers understand how the question of when and how to start benefits can have such a huge impact on their lifetime financial security. In fact, almost none have ever even heard of "Social Security claiming strategy."

Laura and Bob: A Mistake Cost Them Thousands

Recently a couple approached me at a conference where I had spoken on this subject. Laura and Bob are both 67. Laura started to collect her Social Security benefit when she was 63 in the amount of $570 per month; Bob started his when he turned 66 in the amount of $2,200. So far, so good. After hearing me speak, they wondered if there was anything they could or should do to increase their benefits over the long term.

Well, they did have some options that might help them out over the longer term, and I pointed these out. However, something didn't sound quite right: Based on the information they gave me, Laura's benefit should have increased as soon as Bob started to collect his. As it was nearing the end of the month, I told them to call the Social Security Administration for an appointment as soon as they got home from the conference. (The timeliness of your claim matters, one of many factors we'll look into later.)

Sure enough, it turns out that under Social Security's rules Laura should have started collecting $905 a month after Bob filed, an increase of 59%, or $335 more per month. Yet for some reason that adjustment in Laura's favor did not happen. (I suspect it was a side effect of Bob having filed online instead of in person; so much for computers making our lives better…) Once the Social Security Administration corrected Laura's claiming basis, they credited her for six of the 16 months since Bob filed, and an additional $2,010 showed up in her bank account. However, the other earliest 10 months were lost because, well, that's the rule. Laura and Bob are out $3,350 because they were not aware of this earlier.

The Importance of Understanding the System

Actually, Laura and Bob are not dwelling on what was left on the table; they are thrilled to get an entirely unexpected $2,010, plus $335 more per month. That's $4,020 more each year! As Bob later said to me, "Stopping by to see you paid for that conference many times over!"

In fact, it will probably pay off a lot more than that over time. Consider this: If Laura and Bob live to their average life expectancy of 85, they will have collected over $70,000 more, just because they stopped by and asked me a question. Think what a positive impact that can make on their retirement finances.

On the other hand, they might also have never learned about this error. After all, they were already signed up in the system, and there is nothing about that system that would have triggered a review of their claim status without them initiating it. No one from Social Security was ever going to call them up to provide a checkup on their benefits. More likely than not they would have reached age 85 and simply been well over $70,000 poorer. That's the way the system works if you don't understand it.

Laura and Bob did nothing wrong. They followed the rules. They believed all was as it should be. Yet even a well-educated, savvy professional couple like this did not have a clear understanding of something as basic as their Social Security benefits. I wish I could say that the situation of Laura and Bob is rare. It isn't.

Why I Wrote This Book

Social Security is complicated. What most people understand about how it works is simply wrong. That's one reason why I wrote this book: So that when it comes time for you to make what is probably the most important financial decision for the rest of your life—how and when to claim your benefits—you fully understand how to get the most out of what's yours.

The second and most important reason for this book is that I want you to especially understand how to work your benefits to best support an "International Living" life overseas. This is the only book ever written on this subject to address the particular needs of *International Living* readers: how to retire to a better life overseas with greater financial security by wisely managing the Social Security claiming decision. For years *International Living* has educated hundreds of thousands of readers on how affordably you can experience a high standard of living overseas—even on a Social Security check. The purpose of this book is to thoroughly explore the ways that you can get more—much more—out of that check. Social Security pays for a lifetime, adjusted each year for inflation and backed by the U.S. government. That's a combination that can't be beat for providing financial security, especially as we age, when money is the last thing we want to worry about.

Here are some of the important topics we will cover:

- A poor claiming strategy can cost you big time: tens of thousands of dollars in cumulative lifetime benefits for most single people and over $100,000 for married couples—often hundreds of thousands of dollars.

- Why women have the most to gain by understanding claiming strategy.

- Many men inadvertently short-change their wives. They wouldn't if they fully understood the impact of their claiming decisions.

- The Social Security Administration will not provide you advice about when is the best age to start benefits. That's their policy and they stick to it.

- How the Social Security Administration misleads you! The Social Security Administration is your best source for information about your account and what your benefits are or will be in the future, based on your current record. Unfortunately, the Social Security

Administration is not such a good source for information about much else, including how to best manage your account.

- Not all benefits are automatic. For certain benefits you have to both qualify and file in a timely fashion—otherwise you could leave it all on the table, as we saw for Laura and Bob.

- The Social Security Administration rules often don't seem to make sense. For instance, while it can pay to get married, it can be costly under certain circumstances to remarry. Better to live in sin? In some cases the answer is "Yes," at least from a financial point of view.

- Why so many believe that Social Security is about to go bankrupt and why this assumption is so wrong.

As I said, this book is more than an exploration of your Social Security benefits. We will also examine how to incorporate a wise claiming strategy into your overall plans to retire overseas. From a financial point of view, a better life overseas should deliver on these goals:

- You want to live at a higher standard of living than you can afford in the U.S.

- You want to be able to afford to move sooner, not later.

- You want to enjoy greater financial security as you age, without worrying about running out of money.

A well-thought-out claiming strategy can be the key to achieving these goals for financial security in retirement.

Here's a sample of what we'll consider as applied to a life overseas:

- How understanding the way Social Security benefits work gives most people greater confidence to move overseas sooner rather than later.

- How to marshal your assets and talents and use them to support a wise Social Security claiming strategy.

- The most powerful tool in your financial toolbox when you move overseas is the ability to exert far greater control over your expenses.

- Planning for the unexpected: the death of your spouse, health crises, and financial emergencies.

While not every topic may apply to you and your circumstances, my goal is to be sure you can see your situation reflected in enough of the materials that you are empowered to make a wise Social Security claiming decision that serves you throughout your life.

How to Use This Guide

Here's how this book is put together. The first section examines the widespread misconceptions about Social Security that lead so many of us to costly claiming decisions. Most people end up leaving tens of thousands of dollars on the table in cumulative lifetime benefits for singles, and often hundreds of thousands of dollars for married couples. That's a terrible tragedy for most of those people, especially as they get older and are subject to ever-greater worries about running out of money. Not fun for the elderly. I don't want you to be like those people.

The next section will cover Social Security basics that apply one way or another to most people. We'll cover some of the Social Security Administration jargon you need to know (as little as necessary, I promise) such as "Full Retirement Age." You will get insights into what your benefits are worth and understand just how much they increase as you wait to claim. Most importantly, you will learn the best age to start your benefits if you want to get the most out of them. It's actually fairly straightforward for singles. By contrast, it is anything but straightforward for married couples, as well as widow(er)s and divorcees who were married at least 10 years.

Section III brings all these "basics" together in support of an overseas retirement. We examine five different case studies for singles and couples to illustrate how to leverage Social Security claiming strategy to deliver a dream life overseas sooner, rather than later. As we will see, it doesn't matter whether we start with lots of savings or no savings: There is most often a path to a better-quality life starting sooner than we usually think.

Finally, in Chapter 19 we wrap it all up by providing a no-fail, everyone-can-do-this planning tool. We demonstrate how we can use this tool in creating a simple estimate of an affordable spending budget we can rely on to start our adventure overseas. Armed with this information our monthly review of *International Living* magazine becomes even more interesting as we begin to see all the places where we now know—based on the budgeting tool—that we can afford to live. The purpose of the tool is to provide us with concrete steps to transform what we have learned into specific actions. Be sure to check this out.

In the meantime, what you need to know for now is that when we're all done my goal is to give you greater confidence in your financial plans for retirement so you are empowered to make the move sooner rather than later, in greater comfort, and with ever-growing financial security as you age.

About the Author:

Steve Garfink has more than 40 years' work experience in finance, strategic planning, and general management, which provides him with particular expertise in presenting financial concepts to the general public and in financial modeling. He has enjoyed a varied career that included a position as controller for a $50-million multi-year, multi-country regional agronomy and small business U.S. AID development program in West Africa, environmental services management in waste-water treatment facilities, permitting, and on-site remediation, and technology opportunities in security software and vehicle automation. His education includes a BA degree with honors from Yale in International Development Studies and an MBA from Stanford in Finance and Public Management.

Later in his career he turned his financial planning skills to focus on the challenges of retiring baby boomers. It turns out that those boomers who will comfortably enjoy adequate income from a pension and/or their savings make up a small percentage of all boomers, perhaps 15% to 20%. For the rest of us our Social Security benefits will be the principal source of income as we grow older. Yet he quickly learned to his surprise just how poorly informed nearly all of us are about how Social Security benefits work—and more importantly, about how to get the most out of those benefits. Given that financial stability is essential for mental tranquility as we age, he set out to develop learning materials and analytical tools to educate baby boomers—and the generations to follow—about just how valuable our benefits are and how to develop a custom benefit claiming strategy to help us get the most out of them.

Steve founded *Social Security Now or Later* (*http://socialsecuritynowor-later.com/*), to spread his educational message to all baby boomers as well as generations to follow. Then everyone will have the opportunity to understand how to get the most out of his or her Social Security retirement benefits.

More recently he has focused his Social Security educational efforts on people who are looking to spend much or all of their later years living overseas. Most of us can learn to develop a benefit claiming strategy that will provide an unusually high standard of living when we move to any one of a wide number of desirable locations overseas; *International Living* readers are long accustomed to learning about numerous places all over the world where the cost of living is low. Steve wrote this book to provide an education about Social Security claiming strategy in the context of planning for a life overseas.

An avid traveler, Steve and his wife are beginning a new phase in their lives soon—they plan to live for extensive periods in various places overseas, starting in the colonial highlands of Mexico.

NEWS FLASH: SOCIAL SECURITY WILL BE THERE FOR YOU

It has become so common to question the viability of Social Security that it is difficult to know where to begin to push back against the assumption that this vital program is bound to fail. But we must push back, because this wrong-headed belief results in costly mistakes that are destroying the last—and most excellent—chance for baby boomers to establish a financially secure retirement. And once you understand how Social Security really works you can use that knowledge to create the best strategy for the retirement you deserve.

Let's start with the bottom line: The chance is exceedingly small that Social Security is going to run out of money, either for the 10,000 baby boomers starting benefits each day or for the Gen Xers and then Millennials following on their heels. We will look into this in great detail shortly.

In the meantime, let's establish that most baby boomers behave in a way that suggests a considerable lack of confidence in the Social Security program. Many of us—indeed, the vast majority of us, from my experience—live under the delusion that the program is going to run out of money, and unfortunately, we act accordingly. Given the prevalence of negative opinion about Social Security, it's no surprise that so many people claim their benefits early. In 2015, 41% claimed at age 62 and 68% had claimed before reaching Full Retirement Age (currently age 66). Another 22% claim their benefit at Full Retirement Age: That's 90% claiming.[1] Why so many at age 66? Because before this age you may not be allowed to collect benefits if you are still working. (We'll look at these earnings test limits in Section II.)

Younger Generations Trust Social Security Even Less

What's true for baby boomer perceptions of Social Security's financial shakiness is even more exaggerated for the generations that follow. In a recent survey conducted by the Transamerica Center for Retirement Studies, over 80% of survey respondents under age 60 agreed with this statement: "I am concerned that when I am ready to retire, Social Security will not be there for me." And this result was basically the same whether in their 20s, 30s, 40s, or 50s. Among those 60 and older, only 40% agreed—still a high number, although less than half the under-60 rate.[2]

How We'll Dispel the Myth

Nearly all the claiming strategies discussed in this book involve waiting well past age 62 to start your benefits (because it usually results in tens, if not hundreds, of thousands, of dollars more in cumulative lifetime benefits). Yet who is going to wait to claim if they think the program is at risk of running out of money? So before I can wade into the nitty-gritty of claiming strategy, I need to disabuse you of the illusion that Social Security will leave you short-changed. That's the purpose of this section: to address the issues around Social Security's funding head on. If successful, you will come away with a different point of view about the program

---

1   Annual Statistical Supplement to the Social Security Bulletin, 2016, Table 6.A4
2   See "Research Report", Slide 12: *http://www.transamericacenter.org/retirement-research/16th-annual-retirement-survey/social-security-turns-80*

and a great confidence that it will be there not just for you, but for your children and their children.

To that end we will first take a look at the mistaken understanding the public generally shares about the Social Security program—it's running out of money—and the source of that misunderstanding. Then we'll examine the small thread of truth that has been distorted to fuel this faulty belief. Next we'll take a brief look back at some of the history of Social Security, especially a similar time in the past when the program appeared to be running out of money. Hint: We fixed it, no big deal.

That brings us to address these questions: What would it take to fix the current shortfall, and what are the available options? Perhaps more importantly, what will it take for the politicians to come together to reach a compromise? And finally, what will the impact be on the economy if we implement the changes needed to keep the program financially sound for decades into the future? Spoiler alert: There is abundant wealth in the American economy, far more than enough to keep Social Security solvent as far as the eye can see.

Am I Preaching to the Choir?

On rare occasions I run into someone who already shares my confidence that Social Security will be there in full for us. For anyone in that boat, feel free to skip ahead to Section II, "The Fundamentals of Social Security Claiming Strategy." That said, even if you already trust that the program will be there, I invite you to read along in the hope you will be better informed to help others understand why they should plan with confidence on Social Security continuing to pay in full on its promise over the generations. As I said at the start of this section, most people think otherwise, and we need to create an army of voices prepared to push back and spread this more accurate message.

For the rest of you, let me explain why I say that expecting your Social Security benefits to be there in full for you is the smart bet—and that you need to plan accordingly.

If you are a politician and you want to reach out to these voters, which of the following appeals seems, well, more appealing?

"Social Security is fine. Don't worry about it. Please vote for me and send me money."

Or:

"Social Security is going bankrupt. The [FILL IN NAME OF THE OTHER PARTY] Party is out to destroy it. Together we can save it, if you vote for me and send me money."

Just a Way of Grabbing Votes– and Your Money

Unfortunately, pointing to a threat to the primary source of income for most retirees gets far more attention than not. It's a defensible gambit for each of our political parties to accuse the other of conspiring to destroy Social Security. They can easily follow up the accusation with a promise to block such action and protect Social Security, if only you will provide your vote and, of course, send money.

By the way, of the 60 million who receive benefits of some kind, about 57 million of them are of voting age. Consider that, for nearly two-thirds of these beneficiaries, their benefits account for between half and all of their income. They pay close attention to anything that might threaten the biggest single source of their livelihood.[9] In 2014—when Social Security was not an issue on the ballot—32 million of them voted, representing 35% of all votes cast.[10] Imagine how many more would vote if this issue was on the ballot! This provides a vast pool of interested and motivated voters to which the politicians of both parties can return again and again.

9   Ibid., page 8
10 *http://www.census.gov/hhes/www/socdemo/voting/publications/p20/2014/tables.html*, Table 1

How This Explains Our Group Thinking

To recap, politicians speak hysterically about Social Security because it is a reliable path to votes and money. The press repeats the stories because "hysteria" sells more product than "boring." Those directly threatened—the 60 million—fret and stew. Then there are the other couple of hundred million who don't yet collect benefits. What are they to think of all this? Is it at all surprising that all of us are left with the impression of a program that is tottering like a boxer who has taken far too many punches and is about to go down for the long count?

And what should these casualties—these folks suffering the "collateral damage" of this battle of the political parties for loyalties, votes, and money—conclude? If they are close to claiming benefits they could logically figure they had better claim them as soon as eligible and collect before the system runs out of money. The younger "casualties" might understandably conclude that the program isn't going to even be there for them, so why bother to plan for it?

We believe this accurately captures the state and cause of our "group thinking" about Social Security. And it would be fine...if it bears much relation to the truth. But it doesn't. Let's take a look at where the "It's running bankrupt!" talk originates. It's a first step toward getting at the truth about Social Security.

Key Takeaways

There's plenty of talk by politicians and pundits in the public sphere about Social Security...and most of it is negative. Those doing the talking have their own axes to grind and little incentive to talk honestly and thoughtfully about the system. This doesn't keep them from talking. And talking. Don't waste time listening to them: That will only lead to misunderstanding and poor, costly decision-making.

Perfect Weather and Healthy Living on One Social Security Check

By Linda Card, *InternationalLiving.com*

The road leading to the town of Santa Fe de Veraguas climbs gently and steadily up the slopes of the Continental Divide, winding past cattle ranches, jungled hillsides and gurgling rivers. The bright blue roof of the Catholic church in the middle of town is one of the first sights you see. This church marks the center of town. Around it you'll find a soccer pitch, a shaded plaza with benches and a gazebo, and small stores and businesses along the main street.

Horses are common, orchids grow in the wild, rows of coffee plants dot the hillsides, children splash in the rocky streams, and life moves at a relaxed pace.

Santa Fe is a small town in the highlands of Veraguas Province in west-central Panama. It sits at an elevation of about 1,500 feet, providing a cool climate and is surrounded by forested hills and rocky peaks. The weather here is just about perfect.

Daytime temperatures range from 75 F to 85 F and at night you can expect 60s F and 70s F, so it's never sweltering hot nor too chilly. A good fan keeps you comfortable during the day and you may need a light blanket at night. Because it's in the highlands, Santa Fe is cooled by occasional cloud cover and a soft misty rain called *bajareque*, which keeps the area vibrantly green and lush all year round.

This mountain hamlet is off the beaten path and you won't find big-city amenities though you do have modern conveniences such as internet and cellphone services.

But that's exactly the attraction for the retirees and expats who have come from North America, Europe, and other parts of the world. Life here is about healthy rural living. Santa Fe offers year-round warm weather, a low cost of living and unspoiled natural surroundings.

Outdoor activities top the list of things to do, including tubing on the Santa Maria or Mulaba River, hiking along the many trails, visiting the spectacular waterfalls, bird watching, and night-time hikes. Tours of the coffee processing plant and orchid gardens are also popular.

For a big-city fix, the provincial capital, Santiago, is less than an hour's drive on a good highway, and it's a busy commercial center for shopping and taking care of business. A large health center and a new medical facility just east of town provide medical care. A huge shopping mall is under construction and will add many new stores, a cinema, and dining choices for those living in the area.

All of these things drew Bob and Irma Caragol to Santa Fe when they were looking for a retirement home. "We liked Panama after visiting a few times, and were especially attracted to the nice climate and low cost of living in Santa Fe," he says.

They bought a plot bordering the Santa Maria River, hired a local contractor to build the home they designed, and took up full-time residence in 2014. Coming from Albuquerque they initially wanted a higher elevation, but even in Santa Fe Bob's chronic asthma is significantly relieved. "The environment is unspoiled, with clean rivers and no pollution," he says.

Irma enjoys cooking with all the local ingredients, saying, "The food is fresh and healthy, and we eat very well. For a few dollars I can buy two full bags of fruits and vegetables. Our Social Security is more than enough to cover our monthly living expenses, including a part-time gardener."

CHAPTER 2
From a Thread of Truth, a Tapestry of Baloney and Mischief

Let's be clear: The "It's going bankrupt!" talk doesn't happen in a vacuum. It's woven from a thread of truth. We need to identify and understand this "thread" in order to unravel the "whole cloth" of misrepresentations that have shaken the confidence of so many in the Social Security system and deprived them of their dream retirement.

But before we begin, please indulge me while I spill a little background on you. Each year the trustees for Social Security and Medicare update their financial forecasts for these programs. (The trustees and their staff consist of a small army of skilled number crunchers whose assumptions and projections are fully transparent and generally well respected by those of the higher math and statistical echelons.) In preparing these updates the trustees look out 75 years into the future. That's a long time.

Recent forecasts for Social Security indicate that under current assumptions and policy the program will not have enough to pay the full benefits beginning around 2034, about 17 years from now. Instead, the program would have to cut benefits across the board by about 21%.[11] After that, the program is solvent at that payment rate as far as the eye can see. That includes Millennials. Heck, that includes people who aren't even born yet!

21% is the Worst-Case Scenario

Yes, an across-the-board cut of 21% would be painful and shocking (which is why it won't happen—remember those 57 million beneficiaries

---

11 *https://www.ssa.gov/OACT/tr/2016/tr2016.pdf* The 2016 OASDI Trustees Report, page 6

who are of voting age), but that's not at all the same as screaming "Out of money" or "Ponzi scheme" or "Bankrupt!"

No, the worst-case scenario is the 21% cut. (By the way, it is instructive to note that the 2014 Trustees Report projected the shortfall beginning in 2033, a year earlier, and at the rate of 23%.[12] While we can feel grateful for the apparent improvement, the more important takeaway is that these projections are subject to considerable year-to-year variation based on changes in underlying assumptions and the actual performance of the economy.)

Where Were You 20 Years Ago?

Let's look at this forecast in some context. First, we're talking nearly 20 years from now. That's a long time. Consider 20 years ago, the late 1990s. Netscape Navigator burst onto the scene as the preferred internet browser. Most of us still got by with pagers, not cellphones. The U.S. GDP was $7.7 trillion (in current dollars),[13] and the total debt was $5 trillion.[14]

The Dow Jones closed above 5,000 for the first time. The DVD was introduced. The Federal Reserve's prime rate was 8.8%.[15] A gallon of gas was $1.09. Apple Computer was struggling financially, looking to be acquired, and Michael Spindler was at the helm.[16] Michael Spindler?

What's the point of this journey down memory lane? A lot can change in 20 years. While Netscape Navigator basically disappeared, the internet exploded, along with better ways to use it. Steve Jobs returned to head up Apple and brought us iPods, iTunes, iPhones, and iPads. Cellphones are smartphones. We (finally) have the two-way wrist radio that Dick Tracy sported on the comics pages back in our childhood. Amazon, eBay, Facebook, Netflix, and Google (to name a very few) fill needs we didn't even know we had. In 2015 the GDP approached $18.2 trillion (up 140%), and the debt was $19 trillion (up 280%). The Dow is trading around 20,000. The prime rate is 3.25%.

12 *https://www.ssa.gov/OACT/tr/2014/tr2014.pdf* The 2014 OASDI Trustees Report, page 4
13 *http://data.worldbank.org/indicator/NY.GDP.MKTP.CD?page=4*
14 *https://www.treasurydirect.gov/govt/reports/pd/histdebt/histdebt_histo4.htm*
15 *http://www.federalreserve.gov/releases/H15/data.htm*
16 *http://www.thepeoplehistory.com/1995.html*

And much will change in the next 20 years. Most—if not all—of the future is impossible to foresee with much precision.

The Trustees' Forecast Keeps Changing

Second, the trustees' forecast is a moving target. The outcome is based upon numerous assumptions, first and foremost being how the economy and employment perform. For instance, looking at the Trustees Report for 2004, the Social Security retirement account was forecast to run short in 2042; thereafter, benefits would need to be cut by about 25% of scheduled benefits.[17]

Fast-forward 12 years and that deadline has moved up by eight years, to 2034. What happened? Mainly, the Great Recession happened. Social Security gets almost all its funds from the payroll tax, currently 6.2% paid by the employee and a matching amount paid by the employer. (If you are self-employed, you pay both taxes.) In the wake of that devastating recession the unemployment rate doubled to around 10%. With an average of 2% to 3% of people out of the work force, that was 2% to 4% less collected in payroll taxes.[18] Over numerous years that can blow a big hole in the forecast...and it did.

The Trustees weigh numerous other factors, including birth and death (longevity) rates, net immigration, inflation, productivity, and average wage levels. Most don't move as suddenly and unpredictably as employment. Still, they do change over time. For instance, the 1998 Trustees Report forecast "running out of money" in 2032, two years earlier than the latest report. That date moved up to 2042 in the 2004 report because of changes to these other assumptions over time.

In sum, the future forecast is a moving target that changes from year to year with changes in the business cycle and changes in our assumptions about the other factors. What we can conclude with some certainty is that the collections in payroll taxes and other sources of income for Social Security will not be enough to cover benefits beginning sometime in the

17 *http://www.ssa.gov/OACT/TR/TR04/tr04.pdf* Social Security Trustees report for 2004
18 *http://data.bls.gov/timeseries/LNS14000000* Bureau of Labor Statistics

2030s. Further, the shortfall in collections indicate that if nothing else is done, benefits would have to be cut across the board by about 20%-plus for the system to remain in balance over the next 50-60 years.

The 1983 Solution for Social Security

Third, when you consider the origins of the current forecast, what's amazing is just how good it is that there is "only" a forecast shortfall of 21% in the 2030s. Why? The primary elements of the current forecast were set way back in 1983. At that time Social Security was facing a shortfall later that very year, not about 17 years from now, as we stand today.

Ronald Reagan was president. He appointed Alan Greenspan to head a commission to come up with a solution, which they did. President Reagan collaborated with his sometimes-friend House Speaker Tip O'Neill to push the commission's proposals through Congress with strong bipartisan support. Each side of the political aisle had parts it championed and parts it opposed. Each side gave enough to get the deal done.[19]

We will return later to discuss some of the details of this "deal" when we consider what it would take to fix the shortfall looming in 2034. For now, however, we just want to concentrate on the fact that the changes made to the Social Security program by the 1983 legislation were done with the intent of rendering the program solvent far into the future, ideally for 75 years, the planning horizon for the trustees.

The Real Social Security Miracle

Let's stop and contemplate the enormity of that task for a moment. Who among us plans out five, even 10 years into the future? What businesses plan more than a few years into the future? Most businesses have a five-year planning cycle, and most everyone knows those plans are just educated guesses past year two or three. (Life insurance companies and pension managers also have planning horizons spanning decades, but they're a lot like Social Security.)

---

19 http://www.cbpp.org/blog/social-security-its-not-1983

To put it in perspective, in 1983 a plan was created and legislation passed to balance Social Security far off in the future. Today, 34 years later, we peer out into the future and cry, "Oh, we'll be off course by 21% or so in another 20 years if we don't make any course correction!" The truth is, it is simply amazing that a budgeting plan put into place in 1983 is on track to be within about 21% of target 50 years later! In any other sphere of public life the visionaries of 1983 would be hailed as brilliant, the Nostradamus team of the 20th century!

In other words, the looming shortfall in Social Security is less of a growing crisis and more like a miracle in planning: The amazing miracle is that major fixes to the program have not been necessary sooner than this!

Moving to Mexico Allowed me to Quit my Job and Retire Early

By Marcia Gage, *InternationalLiving.com*

After nearly 10 years of marriage, my husband and I decided it was time for a change. We'd lived in a Minneapolis high-rise apartment with spectacular views of the Mississippi River and downtown for seven years, and while we loved our apartment, we didn't love the weather (for six months of the year anyway). And I didn't love my high-stress job or the fact that our cost of living seemed to be getting higher.

We are avid travelers who've been all over the U.S., to Alaska, Canada, Europe, and Asia. But a place we vacationed in many times was Puerto Vallarta, Mexico. We kept going back for the incredible weather, proximity to the U.S. (we can fly directly from Minneapolis in under four hours), and the very reasonable prices for accommodations, food, and the all-important *cervezas*. So we decided it'd be a good place to retire.

Originally, we planned to retire to Mexico when I started collecting Social Security at age 62. But my stressful academic-advisor job was wearing on my physical and emotional health. With my husband, Judd, almost 70, his part-time job as a bouncer was also uncertain. So, we decided to take the plunge and leave shortly before my 61st birthday.

Now, we rent a condo about a 15-minute walk from the center of town and Puerto Vallarta's Bay of Banderas for $800 a month. We have a spectacular mountain view from our rooftop, and get to enjoy the parade of butterflies and hummingbirds on our balcony. This spring we're planning to move closer to town for the shopping convenience and proximity to the ocean and beautiful *malecón*.

Our cost of living in Puerto Vallarta for things like groceries and eating out is about half what we paid in Minneapolis. We've even discovered that we can manage living on our Social Security. We spend about $10 a month on our Mexican cellphones and our rent includes water, internet, gas, and garbage removal.

At the grocery store, we buy local brands which are cheaper than imported U.S. items and often nicer. We often pick up fresh fruit at the little fruit markets. A couple of bananas, a pineapple, and a *jicama* (a root vegetable you can eat with lime and salt, or you can add it to fruit salads) generally costs less than $2. We'd have been lucky to get one pineapple for that in Minneapolis.

Another thing we love about Puerto Vallarta is the excellent food. There are plenty of upscale restaurants here, but we have eaten some of our best meals in the local eateries. Finding where the locals eat is always a good choice for tasty, inexpensive food. One of our favorite places is Travisio's where you can get two big fish tacos for about $3 and a hamburger for the same price. Add a couple of beers and we get lunch for just over $10...including the tip.

It's easy to make friends here too…both with expats and the local people, who are genuinely warm and friendly. Even the teenagers greet me with a *"Buenos dias, senora."* They're also very patient with us and our broken Spanish. It's almost impossible to not make friends here.

Moving to Puerto Vallarta allowed me to quit my stressful job and retire early. Now I have time to indulge in my passions for writing and reading, and enjoy all that this beautiful beach town has to offer.

Why we Won't be Misled by the Politicians

Let's review what we have covered to this point. We noted that, first and foremost, politicians are telling us Social Security is running out of money, going bankrupt, a Ponzi scheme. Upon looking more closely for the justification for these assertions—and based on current projections by the Social Security trustees (and staff)—we find that in fact there will be a shortfall of around 21% between revenues and scheduled benefits in about 20 years. Upon deeper examination we learn that this is not a new discovery; rather, it is the current assessment of a course set in place decades ago. And as we peer further into the distant future we find that we are likely to be slightly off course. Given the massive uncertainties inherent in such a voyage, any reasonable evaluation of the original course settings must conclude the original navigators were near-brilliant. We find we marvel at the accuracy of a set of changes to the program rules put in place 34 years ago that will have kept this mammoth program solvent—not bankrupt or out of money—for about five decades.

Yet others would look at the same set of facts and perform an extreme contortion to twist them into an interpretation that suggests Social Security is going bankrupt, as if the projected shortfall is a sudden revelation and not a well-known fact. And they do so with a straight face! Such are politicians. Unfortunately, their persistence (along with that of a small army of enabling pundits) in trumpeting this misrepresentation of the facts explains the public's general perception that the program is running out of money. This misbegotten belief leads to the early claiming behavior of so many beneficiaries and the general lack of confidence in the program by people of all ages.

Later, we will consider the severe cost to beneficiaries caused by their misunderstanding of solvency of this program. First, though, we'll consider in the next chapter what we did the last time we got off course back in 1983. In Chapter 4 we will follow that with a look at what it might take to get back on course today.

Key Takeaways

To get the skinny on what's actually happening with Social Security we need to glance over the summary at the beginning of the annual Trustees Report. That's where we will find the straight scoop. From their perspective we learn that Social Security is OK, although it is running a bit off course—nothing that a relatively slight course correction won't fix.

CHAPTER 3
Déjà Vu All Over Again: 1983– We Have Been Here Before

As we saw in Chapter 2, it appears that Social Security revenues will become insufficient to cover benefits in the mid-2030s; the current estimate points to a 21% shortfall around that time. While we also saw that the magnitude and year of the shortfall are subject to year-to-year variations, it's a safe bet that we will encounter a considerable shortfall sometime in that timeframe. The proper question to consider is this: What will it take to fix the projected gap between program income and expenses?

To this end it is useful to look back to that time several decades ago when the Social Security program was running up against a shortfall in its balances with important similarities to the one we are now facing. At that time relatively modest changes to the program—course corrections—made a huge difference, as we stated earlier in this book. It is instructive to look at the major elements of the 1983 fix to see what insights it holds for the present. Of course, one big difference between then and now is that while today's shortfall comes to a head in a couple of decades, back in 1983 the program was barreling toward a major shortfall in just a few months—an immediate threat that demanded the attention of the politicians. Nothing like a crisis to focus the mind…

And there's nothing like a crisis to lead to compromise. That was certainly the case in 1983. Republicans were fine with any legislation that didn't raise taxes and Democrats were OK as long as the new law didn't reduce benefits. In the end, each party had to accept a dose of what they didn't want to reach that compromise: new taxes for Republicans and benefit cuts for Democrats.

The Changes Made by the 1983 Legislation

These are the principal changes introduced in the legislation:

➢ Tax Increases:

o On the revenue side the payroll tax was raised gradually over seven years from 5.4% to 6.2% (employee and employer). Consider the impact—about one-tenth of 1% each year—on the pay for someone making $100,000 in today's dollars: Your taxes went up $100 each year, about $2 out of your pay each week, about 5 cents an hour. If that worker got a dollar-an-hour raise each year, 5 cents would go to this tax increase and the rest (after income taxes) into their pocket. The key point is that the increase is phased in gradually—so slowly, in fact, that once the legislation passed, hardly anyone noticed the tiny ding to their paychecks.

o Also on the revenue side, up to 50% of the Social Security benefits for those with higher incomes in retirement became taxable as regular income. Previously, no benefits were subject to federal income tax. (Of course, you could also look at this as a benefit cut, since those who started paying taxes on the benefits effectively had their benefits lowered.)

• In 1993 the threshold for benefit taxation was raised further from 50% to 85% for higher-income beneficiaries.[20] The effect of this change is that in 2014 half of all beneficiaries owed some tax on benefits; about 30% of total benefits paid out were subject to tax.[21]

➢ Benefit Cuts:

o On the beneficiary side, the Full Retirement Age (FRA) was raised gradually from age 65 to 67. How gradually? In 1983 the FRA was 65, as it had been since Social Security was created in 1935. Age 66 applied to those reaching that age beginning in 2009. The age 67 FRA will apply to those reaching that age beginning in 2027.

---

20 *https://www.ssa.gov/history/InternetMyths2.html*
21 *https://www.cbo.gov/publication/49948*

Recall what candidate Reagan said during the 1980 debate, and then look at what he had to say when he signed this legislation into law on April 20, 1983, less than three years later:

"This bill demonstrates for all time our nation's ironclad commitment to Social Security. It assures the elderly that America will always keep the promises made in troubled times a half a century ago. It assures those who are still working that they, too, have a pact with the future. From this day forward, they have our pledge that they will get their fair share of benefits when they retire…

"Our elderly need no longer fear that the checks they depend on will be stopped or reduced. These amendments protect them. Americans of middle age need no longer worry whether their career-long investment will pay off. These amendments guarantee it. And younger people can feel confident that Social Security will still be around when they need it to cushion their retirement."[25]

Take a moment to reflect on President Reagan's statement: "our ironclad commitment to Social Security." He said our elderly shouldn't worry about their benefits, and furthermore the amendments "guarantee" that the career-long investment of the middle aged will pay off. Finally, the program will still be around for younger people. He described this as "a pact with the future." Those are all bold, positive assertions about a Social Security program he intended to be around for the ages. By the way, when this law was enacted the baby boomers were between the ages of 19 and 39, fully into the early part of their working lives as a group, the exact young group for whom he declared "our ironclad commitment" as a "pact with the future."

Thanks to the Nerdy Number Crunchers

Now here's the kicker. The legislators were working in 1983 to close a short-term funding gap through the 1980s of about $400 billion (2015

---

25 Ibid. page 3

dollars) and a projected long-term shortfall equal to about 2.1% of taxable payroll over the 75-year planning horizon.[26] (We will look more deeply into this concept of "percentage of taxable payroll" in the next chapter; for now, we just want to look at some comparative numbers.) The mix of policies finally adopted by Congress was sufficient to solve the near-term problem; over the longer term they forecast solvency in the sense that surpluses in the early decades would be sufficient to cover benefits in the later decades. Note, however, that their forecasts pointed to growing imbalances between program revenue and spending beginning around 2020 that average about -2.6% of payroll during the last 25 years of the plan.[27] Had the surpluses been as big as anticipated in the early years, the program would have run short of funds in the 2050s. Lower surpluses moved that shortfall up by a currently estimated 15 to 20 years.

In other words, the coming negative gap between program income and spending that we see today was actually seen way back in 1983. The only big difference is the planners thought there would be a greater surplus to postpone the day when the gap would need to be filled from other sources (increased taxes or reduced benefits).

So again, we should tip our hats to the nerdy number crunchers over at the Social Security Administration for such an amazing job forecasting the future! The most recent Trustees Report (2016) forecasts the long-term shortfall at 2.58% of taxable payroll if applied today (down from 2.62% in last year's report).[28] Compare that to the near-identical 1983 forecast of 2.6% starting around 2030. We appear to be coming up about 15 years short of the original projections. Still, that's remarkably close for a set of numbers put up 33 years ago.

Think of Social Security as a Boat

To recap the 1983 Social Security funding crisis, 43 years into the program the government faced an immediate shortage of funds to pay benefits if no action was taken. Legislation was passed and signed into

---

26 Ibid. Page 9
27 Ibid. Page 45
28 https://www.ssa.gov/OACT/tr/2016/tr2016.pdf The 2016 OASDI Trustees Report, Page 5

law in May 1983, just averting the crisis and solving the problem for what looked like—and turned out to be good for—many decades.

Given the rather amazing success of the fix done in 1983, what are we to make of the politicians and pundits who rail hysterically today about Social Security's future? Here's one way to look at it. Think of Social Security as a big boat with a lot of folks on board (beneficiaries), with more folks pouring on all the time. People leave only when they pass away. It's smooth sailing. Then some people come along (politicians, mostly) who start to point out to the passengers that the ship is taking on water. Over the coming decades, they proclaim, the water will really start to add up to millions, billions, even trillions of gallons. Something must be done! Some argue to raise the fares for those coming aboard later to fix the holes; others argue to slow down the folks getting on the boat. It is said that if nothing is done, the boat will sink. That can be a huge problem if you are a boat—to say nothing of being a passenger on it…

We Can Fix the Problem
Without Significant Impact

Or at least it can look like a big problem unless you realize just how big the boat is. It's so big that all that water will only slow it down somewhat eventually if nothing is done. Moreover, the holes can be plugged in a number of ways that won't have a significant impact for either those on the boat or those who want to get on some day.

But most people don't understand this about the boat. So they are prone to worry when the politicians spread their hysteria about the holes. Why do the politicians do this? As noted earlier, we suspect they use it for fundraising, declaring they will use our donations to fix the problem. Most of us understand that they will instead use the money to get re-elected. It's what they do.

Today, if nothing is done, current projections indicate we will come upon a funding crisis around 2034, 51 years after the last crisis. Act now and the fixes are less severe; wait until the last second and the fixes will be more dramatic. Either way, we have a good understanding of the scope of the coming problem, as well as of the impact various fixes will have on correcting the problem. In this chapter we looked at the principal steps taken to fix the problem back in 1983 and learned that they were neither drastic nor sudden; rather, they were phased in very slowly over years, even decades, with minimal impact to either beneficiaries or the economy. With this instructive background in mind, in the next chapter we will look at what it will take to implement a fix between now and 2034.

Key Takeaways

It turns out that we faced a looming substantial shortfall in Social Security back in 1983—not unlike the one we face today. The good news is that we came together in a bipartisan manner and fixed it the tried-and-true American way: by compromise with a host of tweaks to the regulations that spread the (mild) pain all around so that it was barely noticed. The bad news: The agreement was reached only mere months before the shortfall would have turned to crisis.

Today the shortfall is nearly 20 years in the future. If history proves the rule, the problem will eventually be fixed. The only question is whether it will be done more gradually and gently (sooner) or more suddenly and harshly (later). Unfortunately, history suggests later… But either way, the fix will get done.

The Cheapest Places to Retire: Five Towns Where You Can Live Better for Less

By the staff of *International Living*

At home, prices are rising. It costs more to put gas in the car, buy groceries, and pay for health insurance. At the same time, retirement savings eroded in the market downturn.

If you're looking overseas for a low-cost alternative to an uncertain retirement at home, there's good news. You can find it in places that offer not just "cheap" living, but a whole basketful of benefits, too—places where a mild spring-like climate is yours all year round…beaches are of powder-white sand…snow-capped mountains soar above colonial towns… and your costs could be as low as $1,000 a month.

In our annual Global Retirement Index (published every January), we rank and rate the best retirement havens in the world. You can stretch your dollars in any of them and live better than you can back home—for less. But the five here offer an outstanding bang for your buck: Ecuador, Panama, Malaysia, Nicaragua, and Mexico.

We asked our editors and in-country correspondents to pinpoint within each nation a specific community to recommend—places that have lots to offer retirees and can be enjoyed on a budget of $1,000 to $2,000 a month.

Santa Fe, Panama: From $1,000 a Month

"*Buenas*," he says, nodding his head as he rides past. Leathery tan on a face framed by a worn cowboy hat, he's the very picture of a Marlboro Man. Except he's Panamanian.

I'm sitting in an ancient Lada Niva—a Russian 4×4 made for rugged terrain. We've stopped so our cowboy (and his herd of cows) can pass safely. It's a chance to take in the view…

In the distance I can see the national park, where hiking trails crisscross hills lush with rainforest. In the treetops above me, I've seen monkeys and toucans and several species of birds I can't name. This is Santa Fe de Veraguas, Panama—a tiny mountain hideaway about 200 miles west of Panama City.

It's the kind of place where $6 will get you a sack of fruit and vegetables…and two chicken breasts for dinner. Where the town's one internet café charges 60 cents an hour and your monthly water bill is rarely over $3. Where home rentals can be as little as $400 a month and any significant crimes take place on TV.

A couple on a budget could live on $1,000 a month in Santa Fe, easy. Expat residents Mitzi and Bill Martain agree. They retired here 11 years ago to live the good life for less. "This was a place where we could live on Social Security, comfortably and happy," says Mitzi.

Santa Fe may boast less English speakers than other, more popular parts of Panama…but the low cost of living is a function of this. You can hire help…cleaning ladies or even builders…for $15 a day. Utilities are low, too. A typical electric bill is maybe $20 a month, internet is as little as $15, and cable starts at about $20. Trash pickup is just $2 a month, and gas for cooking will cost you even less.

Mitzi and Bill are clear about one thing: While the cost of living is great, it's not the only reason they're living in Santa Fe. "We chose to be here primarily because of the people," says Mitzi. "Panamanian people are so wonderful, and will do anything and everything to help you out when they see you're trying to adapt and find your way. We respect and admire them, and we try to earn their respect and admiration, too. It's important to us…especially here in Santa Fe, where there aren't many expats. It's mostly local."

"Include everything…groceries and going out to restaurants…my weekly shopping trips to Rivas (a nearby town)…and our monthly shopping trips to Managua and hotels and restaurants there…and even gas for the car…all we spend is $1,000."

They both laugh and Ralph says again for emphasis: "Our monthly expenses are just $1,000…. a *thousand* dollars. We actually have money left over each month from our Social Security…so every October we take a cruise."—*Suzan Haskins.*

Campeche, Mexico: From $1,400 a Month

Just 100 miles south of Mérida on Mexico's Yucatán Peninsula, Campeche has long been under the radar for expats. But that is changing fast as visitors discover the charms of this city, considered one of the safest in Mexico.

Campeche is one of Mexico's few World-Heritage cities to sit by the sea—it's right on the Gulf of Mexico. A three-mile-long *malecón* (boardwalk), with running and cycling paths, mini-park spaces, and workout equipment, runs beside the water. Just a few blocks inland lie the city's World-Heritage neighborhoods and historic center, with their rows of attractive candy-colored, Spanish-colonial facades.

The historic center (just eight blocks square) and the three historic neighborhoods are walkable, and it's possible to live in these areas without a car. Campeche has a small-town or even village feel—remarkable in a city of almost 300,000.

The government—both state and national—has made improvements in the area over the last few years. The highway to Mérida is now four lanes, reducing driving time to less than one-and-a-half hours. A new shopping mall just off the *malecón* is anchored by the high-end Liverpool department store. It also has a Cineplex, restaurants, and a range of stores. Campeche already has a Walmart Super Center, a Sam's Club, and numerous large supermarkets, plus a large traditional market just outside the historic center. In addition, more of the historic center has been made pedestrian-only, with art and sculpture exhibits decorating public spaces and outside dining available.

"The weather is good, the people are friendly, and there are fresher fruits and vegetables year-round here than you get back home," says expat Daniel Record, of life in Campeche.

Day-to-day expenses are relatively low. You can buy a week's worth of fruits and vegetables at the market for as little as $8. A sandwich or tacos from one of the many small *loncherías* (lunch joints) will cost you $2 to $3, while a seafood plate at a sit-down restaurant may run $12 or $15.

You can rent a small local house for as little as $400 a month. Comfortable modern homes, with two or three bedrooms, rent unfurnished for $500 and up. These same homes sell from $150,000.

Colonial properties, which most expats want, cost more. Unrenovated colonials for sale start at about $80,000—most cost more. Relatively few renovated colonials are on the market, but you can get small ones starting at around $100,000. Likewise, only a handful of furnished, renovated colonials are available. Colonial rentals in the *centro* and historic neighborhoods generally rent for $800 and up. Modern rentals, and colonials outside the center can start as low as $300 a month. More colonial rentals are desperately needed; it's a business opportunity looking for an entrepreneur…
—*Glynna Prentice.*

Vilcabamba, Ecuador: From $1,485 a Month

Johnny Lovewisdom, a quirky spiritual seeker, first put Vilcabamba, Ecuador on the gringo map in the 1960s. He advocated (among other beliefs) breatharianism—that one can live on air and sunshine alone. (He died in 2000…some say of malnutrition.)

While clean air and constant sunshine are abundant in this lush valley in southern Ecuador, so is fresh, organic food. The healthy lifestyle is just one reason expats are drawn to Vilcabamba today.

Many residents live to be 100 years old or more. That may be thanks to clean water, clean, stress-free living, or the near-perfect climate. Just shy of the equator and at an elevation of 5,000 feet, temperatures average between 65 and 81 F, day in and day out. Estimates put the number of permanent foreign residents at about 150 and part-timers at perhaps another 100.

Although it takes some doing to get to Vilcabamba, it's a small price to pay. Literally. Vilcabamba is among the lowest-priced retirement havens in the world.

Here is a sample monthly budget for a couple in Vilcabamba:

Housing (rental of a furnished two-bedroom apartment or home): $375

Utilities (including phone, water/electricity, internet, and DirecTV): $155

Maid (once a week): $60

Groceries (not including alcohol): $400

Maintenance and fuel for one car: $140

Misc. (personal items, etc.): $75

Entertainment (two people dining out six times per month, with drinks, dessert, tip): $200

IESS (social security) healthcare: $80

Monthly Total: $1,485—*Suzan Haskins.*

Penang, Malaysia: From $2,000 a Month

My wife and I first came to Penang, Malaysia for a vacation in 2008 and after two weeks, which we extended to three, decided that it was the perfect place for us to live. From the region's best street food to smart restaurants, bars, shopping malls, and movie theaters, it had everything that we needed and more.

George Town, Penang's capital, is a UNESCO-listed city and dates from 1786. Most of the buildings in town were built between 1820 and 1900, and it's these historic streets that are the main attraction for visitors to the island. Some of the colonial mansions on Penang Hill were built even earlier. We loved its history, but also its deserted white-sand beaches, pristine jungle trails, constant sunshine, and affordability.

There is a lively street culture anchored in religious festivals, a recently opened performing arts center at Straits Quay Marina, and events like the Penang World Music Festival and the annual George Town Festival (a month of performances) that have become a must-see event in Asia.

Our apartment is a short distance from the local market, where we can buy vegetables, fruits, bread, meat, seafood, and all manner of goods. An entire bagful of fresh fruit, including mangoes, bananas, apples, oranges, and pineapples, costs just $6.

High-speed internet is reliable and costs $30 a month, and the premier cable TV package for $40 includes favorites like HBO, CNN, numerous sports and movie channels and the BBC.

We live in a spacious 2,100-square-foot apartment with four bedrooms and three bathrooms. We also have a covered carport, swimming pool, and well-equipped gym. The apartment is fully air conditioned and fitted with ceiling fans, and costs $900 a month. We have a maid who comes one day a week and costs just $56 a month.

Penang is known internationally for its good medical care, which is downright cheap. Six world-class hospitals are situated within George Town. All the medical staff speak perfect English. You don't need to make an appointment to see a specialist and seeing one can cost as little as $12.

Originally from San Francisco, Ivan Peters has been living in Penang for just over two years. He noticed that three moles on his back had changed color, and he decided to have them removed. The initial consultation by a world-class plastic surgeon cost him $12, and the moles were removed five minutes later. The total cost came to $22. In the U.S. he estimates that that it would have cost closer to $1,000.

Penang is an exciting place to live and we have no regrets about moving here. Well, just one…that we didn't do it years ago. Where else could you eat out seven nights a week, sampling any cuisine you want, and still live for under $2,000 a month?—*Keith Hockton*

CHAPTER 4
How to Fix the Coming Social Security Shortfall

Many people will tell you that Social Security is doomed to fail, that it's headed for bankruptcy. But that simply isn't the truth, although the system does need a few tweaks to keep it going into the future. Social Security can provide you with the income you need for retirement, and by knowing how to best utilize this resource, you can attain a better retirement lifestyle than you even thought.

We have seen what it took to fix a major looming shortfall in the Social Security program balances in 1983. In this chapter we look at what it will take to fix the projected shortfall coming in the 2030s.

As the old saying goes, if you want to fix something you first have to measure it. To this end we will begin by looking at the principal measurement used by the Social Security trustees to quantify the shortfall. Then we will consider that measurement in the context of some recent cuts and increases in Social Security taxes (part of the American Recovery and Reinvestment Act of 2009). With that background we can turn to consider five of the major fixes that are continuously evaluated to fix the problem. Finally, we will look into our crystal ball and imagine what an eventual fix might look like.

Measuring the Shortfall

As we learned in Chapter 2, since the start of the Social Security system the trustees have been required to provide an annual report on how the program is doing financially. The trustees basically answer this question: How long can we continue to pay full benefits based on current laws, payroll tax rates, and projections of employment, population, and economic growth? Generally, the trustees peer 75 years out to the future, adding a year with each new report to maintain the 75-year outlook.

While the trustees use a number of measures to assess the stability of the program, the primary measure is "percentage of taxable payroll." (As you may recall, we touched briefly on this subject back in Chapter 3, promising to revisit it in more detail later. That time has come.)

The "payroll" component of this measure consists of all the wages, salaries, commissions, and so forth paid to workers—whether employed by someone else or self-employed—over the course of a year. The "taxable" part reduces the total "payroll" by a bit because (1) some people (primarily government workers in 15 states) have a separate pension system and do not participate in the program,[29] and (2) there is a limit to the Social Security taxes that you have to pay in any given year (called the "maximum earnings subject to Social Security taxes").

So the "taxable payroll" is any income on which payroll tax is collected. For every dollar you earn up to the limit, you have 6.2% of your income paid to Social Security and your employer (or you, if you are self-employed) chips in a matching 6.2% for a total of 12.4%. (However, if you are among the 6% of workers who earn above the maximum earnings subject to Social Security taxes—$127,200 in 2017—[30]you and your employer no longer pay this tax for earnings over this limit, no matter how much you earn.)

Each year the Social Security trustees look to determine what percentage of this "taxable payroll" they would need to collect in order for the program to remain in balance over various time horizons based on current assumptions. In their most recent report they project that the shortfall is 2.66% of taxable payroll through the next 75 years to 2090.[31] In other words, all else being equal, the payroll tax would have to be 1.33% higher for each of the employee and the employer, 7.52% each instead of 6.2% each, in order to balance the program through 2090.

---

29 http://www.nea.org/home/16819.htm
30 https://www.ssa.gov/news/press/factsheets/colafacts2017.pdf
31 https://www.ssa.gov/OACT/TR/2016/tr2016.pdf The 2016 OASDI Trustees Report, page 71

We Raised the Tax 2% in 2013... and the Sky Did Not Fall!

Shortly we are going to look at a considerable number of program changes that could be made in order to fix the projected shortfall; increasing the amount of the payroll tax is only one among many. However, before wading into that discussion let's do a brief thought exercise to get a better sense of how it would "feel" to the typical taxpayer (and to the greater economy) to fix the problem solely by raising taxes. Just how drastic would the impact be?

As it turns out, we had a recent experience of roughly this size of tax increase. As part of the stimulus package enacted into law during the Great Recession, the payroll tax rate collected from workers was reduced from 6.2% to 4.2% beginning in 2011 and extended through 2012. The impact of this 2% cut was to put just over $100 billion into the economy for each of those two years.[32] In a $15 trillion economy the magnitude of the impact was small;[33] still, it had the desired stimulus effect since most of this tax cut was spent by the workforce.

Let's look at it from the viewpoint of the typical worker. The tax cut effectively put 2% more back into every worker's pocket. If you were earning $52,000 a year, your paycheck increased by $20 a week. If you made $104,000 a year, you got an extra $40 a week in your pocket.

Do You Remember Your Stimulus Cut?

Think back to 2011 and 2012, especially if you were in the workforce. Did you celebrate that extra money? Did you go all wild and crazy and think you had hit the big time? Or did that $10, $20, $40—whatever your amount was per week—just disappear into the pile of bills along with all your other money? Did you even notice the amount of your increase? Or was it just a blip in your finances that hardly registered?

---

32 *http://www.ncpa.org/pub/ba780*
33 *http://www.bea.gov/national/*

1. **Increase the Full Retirement Age (FRA).** As we saw earlier, this was one of the measures used to solve the projected shortfall back in 1983. Originally, the FRA was set at 65. This was changed gradually from 65 to 67 as part of the 1983 legislation. In fact, it was so gradual that the first beneficiaries subject to the age 67 FRA are those who reach that age in 2027, 44 years after the law was passed. Or, put another way, those folks were 23 years old at the time of enactment: plenty of time for these future beneficiaries to adjust their retirement plans accordingly.

There's an important takeaway from this example that gives insight into how any future changes are likely to be applied: gradually. Put another way, the closer you are to starting your benefits, the less likely that any changes will be applied to you.

Let's look at some recent evidence to support this. As of this writing, it is early days in the Donald Trump presidency. Still, we can already detect the range of options up for consideration. On the one hand, President Trump took the position early in his campaign stating: "I was the first & only potential GOP candidate to state there will be no cuts to Social Security, Medicare & Medicaid. Huckabee copied me."[34] When asked later in the campaign whether he stood by his intention to raise the Full Retirement Age to 70, as expressed in his book, *The America We Deserve* (2000), he replied:

> Yeah, not anymore because now what I want to do is take money back from other countries that are killing us and I want to save Social Security. And we're going to save it without increases. We're not going to raise the age and it will be just fine.[35]

He continued to maintain this position throughout the campaign.

On the other hand he appointed to key positions staunch supporters of raising the retirement age. For instance his selection to direct the Office of Management and Budget, Rep. Mick Mulvaney (R-S.C.), is a longtime advocate for raising the retirement age

---

34 Twitter, @RealDonaldTrump, 8:38 AM - 7 May 2015
35 *http://www.cbsnews.com/news/donald-trump-60-minutes-scott-pelley/*

to 70, along with other changes that would effectively fix Social Security through benefit cuts. During his confirmation hearings he acknowledged that his position is somewhat at odds with the president, though he emphasized that he would not propose any changes that would reduce benefits for current beneficiaries.[36]

Let's review this range of conservative positions on raising the retirement age: President Trump wants to keep it the way it is, while his Budget Director Mick Mulvaney is a proponent of raising the FRA for future beneficiaries. If this is the conservative range of opinion, you can imagine what the liberal position will be! My point is that change in whatever form it takes is likely to be gradual on any changes that impact large numbers of people. (As for changes that affect a relatively small number of beneficiaries, that's another matter we will examine shortly.)

By the way, the base argument for raising the retirement age is that overall the population is in fact living longer. The base case against it is that these gains in longevity fall almost entirely to the more affluent. Workers engaged in the manual trades and who often earn less are more likely to die younger. Raising the retirement age would place an unfair hardship on them. There are no simple answers to these issues. Most of us believe it is the job of the politicians to reach a fair and judicious compromise.

2. **Change how the annual cost of living adjustment (COLA) is calculated.** This can get deep in the wonk weeds pretty fast, but for those of you who are interested I'll take a stab at it. The current COLA is based on an analysis of a relatively fixed basket of goods and services that are monitored constantly for price changes and captured in the Consumer Price Index (CPI). If the price of apples goes up or down, the CPI increases accordingly.

Another method proposed for calculating the COLA is based on what's called Chained CPI. Under Chained CPI if the price of

---

36 "Nominee to head budget office defends support for cuts to Social Security, Medicare", Ylan Q. Mui, *The Washington Post*, January 24, 2017

apples goes up an assumption is made that at some point consumers will buy fewer apples and switch to something cheaper: pears or oranges perhaps. Thus the overall cost of living doesn't increase as much. In practice the Chained CPI goes up roughly 10% less than the regular CPI.[37]

In fact this change was proposed in President Obama's budgets earlier in his administration. It was dropped in later years following protest by senior lobbies including AARP. These groups argue that retirees actually experience higher-than-average increases in their cost of living because of ever-rising healthcare costs that make up an ever-growing part of their spending as they age.

3. **Change the way benefits levels are tied to average wages.** Most people are unaware of this feature of how our benefits are determined, so it is worth spending a moment to understand it. Those workers who reach age 60 in any given year have their future benefit amount tied to the average prevailing wage in that year. Thereafter the COLA adjustments preserve that level of purchasing power during the remainder of their retirement. Over time average wages increase substantially, so much so that the benefit you will eventually receive will be much greater in constant dollars than the benefit your parents or grandparents receive.

Consider an example based on the last two generations of retirees compared to those retiring today. In order to compare apples to apples, we'll use the maximum possible benefit in a given year, based on someone who earned at or above the earnings limit most of their working life. We start with a worker born in 1920. They reach their Full Retirement Age—age 65 for them—in 1985. If they are alive in 2015 at the age of 95, the benefit would be about $1,750 after all the COLA adjustments since 1985.[38]

Now imagine this worker's child, born in 1945 when the parent is 25 years older. The child reaches their FRA of 66 (remember, the

---

37 *https://www.ssa.gov/oact/solvency/provisions/summary.html* Summary of Provisions That Would Change the Social Security Program based on the 2015 Trustees Report, A3.
38 Maximum FRA benefit starting 1985: *https://www.socialsecurity.gov/policy/docs/statcomps/supplement/2010/2a20-2a28.html#table2.a27* Table 2.A28; COLA amounts: *https://www.ssa.gov/OACT/COLA/colaseries.html*

FRA was increased gradually from 65 to 67 as part of the 1983 fix) in 2011. Their FRA benefit in 2015, after COLA adjustments, is about $2,366.[39] Recall that both paid in at the maximum, yet in 2015 (and assuming both are still alive) the child receives 35% more than the parent.

Suppose both chose to wait to age 70 to start their benefits in order to maximize their benefits. Based on the rules that apply to their respective birth years, the parent would receive $2,012 in 2015; the child, $3,123 or 55% more.

Let's carry our comparison into another generation for a grand-child born in 1970 who reaches FRA in 2037 at age 67. If the same rates of increase of 35% over the 25-year difference in age apply, their benefit would be $3,194 in 2015 dollars. Waiting to age 70 to start benefits would yield a monthly benefit of $3,961 in 2015 dollars. The grandchild's benefit is almost double the grandparent's age 70 benefit in just two short generations.

Birth Year	Age in 2015	FRA	FRA Benefit*	Age 70 Benefit*
1920	95	65	$1,750	$2,012
1945	70	66	$2,366	$3,123
1970	45	67	$3,194	$3,961
*In constant 2015 dollars				

Some argue that the level of benefits is getting too rich this way and that modifying the formula to increase the level less than the full increase in wages would be appropriate. Making an adjustment in the rate of increase—depending on the magnitude—would sub-stantially reduce future liabilities under the program.

---

39 *https://www.ssa.gov/policy/docs/chartbooks/fast_facts/2011/fast_facts11.pdf* Page 2

Possible Changes to Social Security	Impact as % of Taxable Payroll	Long-range Shortfall Eliminated
A3 – Base COLA on Chained CPI Beginning December 2017	0.55%	21%
B2.1 – Adjust Benefit for Longevity Increases Near Retirement	0.53%	20%
C1.1 – Increase FRA to 68 by 1 Month Each 2 Years Starting 2022	0.36%	13%
E1.8 – Increase Tax Rate by 0.6% by 2024 from 12.4% to 13%	0.54%	20%
E3.1 – Increase Taxable Maximum to 90% of Earnings by 2026	0.77%	29%
Total Impact as a Percentage of Taxable Payroll	2.75%	103%

Source: Summary of Provisions That Would Change the Social Security Program Based on the 2016 Trustees Report — *https://www.ssa.gov/oact/solvency/provisions/summary.html*

The columns on the right show the current estimate of the impact of the referenced change on the long-term financial stability: (1) as a percentage of taxable payroll and (2) as a percentage that the change contributes to eliminating the projected long-term shortfall. You will recall that the 2016 Trustees Report estimates that the long-range shortfall is equal to 2.66% of taxable payroll. The first change in the table, implementing a Chained CPI (as we discussed earlier in this chapter), would reduce the long-range shortfall of 2.66% by about 0.55%, to 2.11%. Put another way, the impact of that change eliminates 21% of the long-range shortfall (as reflected in the last column).

The second change in the list slightly reduces the rate at which benefits increase with increases in wages (by basing the retirement benefit to wage increases as of four years prior). The third increases FRA from age 67 to age 68 over 24 years. The fourth increases the tax rate from the current 6.2% (for employee and employer) to 6.5% over a six-year period; the increase would reduce pay by about $1 more per week each year reaching

$6 per week in the sixth year for someone earning $100,000. The last change increases the taxable maximum (currently $127,200—no Social Security tax is due for income earned above that level) to capture 90% of all earned income; this merely restores this rate of income capture to the same percentage that was captured at the time the 1983 amendments were put in to place.

As you can see in the table these changes would combine to eliminate the long-range shortfall 75 years into the future. As you can also see all of these changes phase in gradually and have modest impacts on any demographic group. Yet these "tweaks" to the program carry enormous impact: Everyone pays or gives up a little to ensure that the Social Security program is sound well into old age for today's seniors as well as for those babies being born this year.

What Keeps us from Making These Changes?

The biggest challenge is getting the political stars to align in order to reach an overall compromise such as was done in 1983. Once the politics are put aside, what would it take to reach that compromise, given all the possible alternatives? Here's the take from one who might know because he led the committee that developed the fixes to the problem back in 1983: Alan Greenspan. His comments from 2006, as reported by the Associated Press, are instructive:

> Discussing the strain of entitlement programs on the nation's long-term fiscal health, Alan Greenspan said Medicare is much more of a problem and harder to deal with than Social Security.

> "If you get beyond the political rhetoric" and assembled a group to solve Social Security, "it would take them 15 minutes. It would take them 15 minutes only because 10 minutes was used for pleasantries," he quipped. The audience—people attending the Commercial Finance Association meeting—erupted in laughter.[42]

Ah! The problem is the "political rhetoric." Why are we not surprised?

---

42 *http://usatoday30.usatoday.com/money/economy/2006-10-27-greenspan_x.htm* Associated Press, USA Today online, October 27, 2006

What is Likely to Happen?

If, as Alan Greenspan asserts, it would take less than 15 minutes to solve Social Security's problems, how soon might such a meeting be arranged? Well, as we learned in Chapter 3—and as Mr. Greenspan could tell us—the last time the Congress did a big fix was in 1983, when he led such a committee. At that time insolvency was approaching in a matter of months, and the politicians of both parties moved diligently to avoid the looming cliff.

Standing here 32 years later it doesn't look like much has changed. Nothing seems to get done by Congress absent a crisis (like the 2008 recession) or a deadline (like each time Congress has to increase the debt limit). Brinksmanship is the game of the times. This is unfortunate because putting a fix in place soon makes it possible for the changes to be the most gradual thereby allowing everyone plenty of time to adjust. Not likely to happen this way…

As a case in point, look at the Bipartisan Budget Act of 2015[43] passed in November of that year. Given the heightened level of conflict that paralyzes our recent politics, the stars aligned briefly in October and this bill set modestly increased spending authority for the next two years. This agreement was driven by the desire of enough members of both parties to avoid serious conflict for the next two years until after last year's presidential election: the proverbial kicking of the can down the road. Job accomplished.

Here's how this is a case in point for our purposes: a handful of urgent, if not directly related, items were crammed into this bill as well. First, they raised the debt limit, which was on the brink of being breached. Second, they fixed the Social Security Disability fund, which was going to run out of money in 2016. They fixed it by essentially taking money out of the Social Security retirement reserve accounts, which are far better funded in the near term, so not really a fix at all, just a postponement of the reckoning. However, had they failed to fix it, disability benefits would

---

43 *https://www.govtrack.us/congress/bills/114/hr1314/text*

have been cut for 9 million beneficiaries[44] by an estimated 19% within a year or less.[45] Third, the act fixed a quirk in the Medicare law that was about to levy a punishing Part B premium increase of 55% on about one-third of beneficiaries while the other beneficiaries got hit with no increase. Congress in its wisdom (such as it is) knew that such a situation would produce a furious outcry by a projected 16 million[46] (voters) starting in January 2016. Congress will do almost anything to avoid a furious outcry. In sum, several crises coming to a head in a matter of days, months or the following year were dealt with by slipping them into this budget legislation without actually addressing the underlying problems. Instead, our legislators found ways of putting these off to deal with later.

Why Congress Won't Take Drastic Measures

These fixes offer compelling evidence for why Congress will find a way to fix the looming shortfall in Social Security benefits coming in the 2030s. In the face of the prospect of (unfairly) raising Part B premiums on one-third of Medicare beneficiaries, Congress blinked fast and rolled back the increase from about $50 per month, $600 per year, to about $15 per month. (Other beneficiaries will be subject to this increase in subsequent years.) That's what Congress did when facing a relatively modest premium change that would have taken $50 per month out of the pockets of 16 million beneficiaries. Now imagine the prospect of cutting Social Security benefits across the board by over 20% sometime in the 2030s—for more than 75 million retirees.[47] On the average monthly benefit today of $1,341,[48] that would be a cut of over $275 per month, $3,300 per year. That's over five times greater than the Medicare premium increase would have been, and it would affect five times as many people. Imagine the outcry. Then imagine Congress finding a way to avoid it. Not so hard to imagine, is it?

All of which is not to say that Congress won't make occasional abrupt and punishing changes to the Social Security program. As a case in point, the 2015 Bipartisan Budget Act eliminated certain claiming strategies

44 https://www.ssa.gov/oact/STATS/dibStat.html
45 https://www.ssa.gov/oact/trsum/
46 http://www.usnews.com/opinion/economic-intelligence/2015/10/29/budget-deal-stops-medicare-premium-spike-but-not-forever
47 https://www.ssa.gov/news/press/basicfact.html
48 https://www.ssa.gov/news/press/factsheets/colafacts2016.html

that will cost tens of millions of married couples in which the younger spouse turns 62 in 2016 or later to potentially lose out on $10,000 to over $60,000 in benefits. This has come as a shock to many who are within just a few years of retirement and who had planned on those benefits, leaving little time to adjust to the loss. The key difference is in the number of beneficiaries who are likely to be affected by any given change—and be aware of it; in this case the legislators perceived—apparently accurately—that there were not enough voters who would kick up a fuss over the changes because they never knew that this option existed. (Still, over 10 million were grandfathered into this benefit. You can determine whether you might qualify in Chapter 10.)

Let's recap what we've covered in this chapter. First, we reminded ourselves that we raised Social Security taxes from 4.2% to 6.2% (that's a 48% increase!) in 2013 and the sky didn't fall. (Of course, that was after we cut the tax to 4.2% from 6.2% in 2011 in order to stimulate the economy…so we were just setting it back to where it was.) Then we looked at some of the various ways to shore up the Social Security program: the "tweaks." These include increasing the Full Retirement Age gradually, changing the method for calculating the annual cost of living adjustment, means testing of benefits, raising the tax rate (though not as much as the 2013 bump from 4.2% to 6.2%), and raising the tax cap so that high-income earners pay the tax on more of their income.

Nearly all the people I discuss these "tweaks" with agree that they are indeed "tweaks." And, as we will see shortly, the party leaders agree as well. And most people I discuss this with agree that it shouldn't be that difficult to find a compromise by which everyone gets a little of what they love and a little of what they hate and Social Security is made solvent once again many decades into the future beyond 2034.

We introduced the final section of this chapter as a speculation on how our federal lawmakers are likely to fix the looming shortfall in benefits. Sadly we must conclude that we should not hold our breath waiting for today's politicians to address this problem anytime soon, not when it won't be a crisis until sometime in the 2030s. In the meantime we will have to take heart from the steady pattern of political behavior on this subject. When push does eventually come to shove, the politicians will resolve the shortfall without significantly penalizing anyone. As we saw in this chapter there are plenty of alternatives that can spread the pain around in such a manner that no age group is hit too hard and any changes are introduced gradually over a period of time.

So why don't the politicians get together to hash it out and be done with it? Sadly, it doesn't appear to be how they operate. They appear to be at their best when there is a crisis or deadline. Need to fund the government for the next fiscal year? Congress gets it done. Sometimes it's a couple of weeks late and most federal workers are furloughed during that period. All times (so far) they allocate money to pay the furloughed workers anyway.

Need to raise the debt limit? Again, so far it gets done—although not without inordinate carrying on and threats and bluster by the right and the left. Similarly, an eventual fix for Social Security will eventually get done. Unfortunately for all those worried about their benefits in the meantime, it probably won't happen until the last minute. There's nothing like a crisis to focus the attention and get the necessary work done. But until the crisis, endless baloney about Social Security's finances seems unavoidable.

Key Takeaways

Based on current estimates there is a shortfall of around 21% in the Social Security finances that will materialize in the early-to-mid 2030s. A range of "tweaks" to the regulations that will close the shortfall is reasonably easy to identify: a mix that combines modest revenue increases with modest benefit reductions spread out over a number of years to minimize the impact. A similar fix was enacted into law in 1983 to stabilize the program back then. Comparable changes will be needed some time in the next 20 years or so. The only question is when—not if—the politicians will sit down to find a judicious compromise.

Living a Fulfilling Life in Nicaragua on a Social Security Check

By Bonnie W. Hayman, *InternationalLiving.com*

San Diego native Robert Quartiano, 63, started his work life at 18 as a commercial fisherman in Oregon. At 40, he thought he was getting a little old for the job so he went to school and became a registered nurse. Nineteen years later, at 59, Robert decided to retire early.

Robert had visited Nicaragua in 2002 and liked the fact that it was so economical to live there. But what really sold him on Nicaragua were the property prices. He bought a lot (a little less than an acre) with a small shack for $17,000. Located about five miles north of the beach town of San Juan del Sur, he decided to build his dream house there.

Robert liked the funky town of San Juan del Sur, with its collection of restaurants, clothes and surf shops, colorful characters, and the fact that it is surrounded by 22 beaches. But he wanted his dream house to be far from the noise and high energy of the town.

"My retirement life in San Diego wasn't fulfilling enough for me. I lived in a condo, the HOA rules prevented me from being able to do anything, any hobby. I could go to the beach, but I grew up there and had been to these places thousands of times. Maybe if I'd had a big home with landscaping projects and other things to fix, it would have been okay. But I couldn't afford a house that big there," says Robert.

In Nicaragua, Robert has multiple landscaping projects and is adding more to his dream house. Labor is extremely affordable. A cement mason in Nicaragua costs $17.85 a day…a lot less than what it could cost in the U.S.

And he is able to live in Nicaragua and continue building his home all using only his Social Security check.

Robert says, "I get $1,000 a month on Social Security. My property taxes come to $60 a year. Electricity is $9 per month and water $36. I don't have WiFi or TV. I use my smartphone when I need to communicate with people and for WiFi, I go to the nearby Villa Mar Hotel/Restaurant and get it for free with my $3.65 breakfast or I pay for it when I need it ($1 for an hour). Sometimes I go to Mango Rosa, an expat community, with a pool and restaurant to eat lunch. I also buy my fruits, vegetables, and chicken from the local fruit truck twice a week."

Robert built his dream house five miles north of the beach town of San Juan del Sur.

And a new little store, Rancho Maria's, recently opened near his home that has "gringo" things. Think parmesan cheese, olive oil, bacon, Canada Dry club soda, black and green olives, and more.

"I don't get sick that often; the one time I used healthcare I had severely sprained my ankle. At the public hospital in Rivas there was no paperwork involved and the doctor saw me within a minute. No blood test, no checking a million things before they take care of the problem. He gave me an X-ray to ensure that my ankle wasn't broken, made a removable soft cast, wrote a prescription for pain pills, and when I went to pay, I was told it was free," says Robert. Nicaragua, like many countries in the world, has government-subsidized healthcare.

"I have someone to clean my house twice a week for three hours and a gardener five days a week for three hours, and spend $300 on food, a couple of bottles of rum, and some breakfasts, lunches, and dinners out," says Robert of his monthly budget.

"My day is simple. I wake up at 4 a.m. I read until the sun rises at around 5:20 a.m. I sweep out the kitchen, then relax and have my first cup of coffee. My tools are in the kitchen and I like to have a project ready to go each day. I'll do landscaping, pruning, or plane wood to detail the barbecue area. I create lawn art, take out the weeds, or take a walk to look at monkeys. My day is filled with things I want to do and love to do. So different from San Diego where life often seems to get in the way," says Robert.

Robert has advice for people who are thinking of moving to Nicaragua: "Come for a visit first to see if you like the tropics; this climate is not for everybody. Check out the neighborhood you're interested in. You might find out that there's a dog that barks every night, or a rooster crowing, or pigs that show up inside your property. But you might discover the retirement location of your dreams."

CHAPTER 5
Why Social Security Will be Fixed

If you know the best strategy for getting the most out of your Social Security benefits, you can grant yourself a better retirement than you might have thought possible. However, many people will tell you that Social Security is doomed.

In the last three chapters we've considered ways to secure Social Security based on acting now (about 20 years before it runs into a shortfall) instead of waiting to fix it closer to the last minute. The fact is the last time we did a big fix was in 1983, when legislation was passed and signed a mere 10 days before a shortfall would start. And either way, the odds are that a deal will get done that basically shores up the program far into the future. Why? Two facts conspire to ensure that Social Security will continue to pay scheduled benefits in full now and far into the future: The program is exceedingly popular and our economy can easily afford it. Let's look at each of these facts in turn.

Social Security provided 65 million people with benefits in 2015, around 20% of the U.S. population of more than 300 million.[49] About 85% of the benefits paid went to retired workers 62 and older, their spouses, children, and survivors.[50] The rest went to disabled workers, average age 54.[51]

How Does the Election Cycle Affect Social Security?

Consider that in any given election those who are older vote at a far greater rate than younger voters do. For example, in the November 2014

49 *https://www.ssa.gov/policy/docs/chartbooks/fast_facts/2016/fast_facts16.pdf* Page ii.
50 Ibid. Page 15
51 Ibid. Page ii

election cycle 42% of citizens voted. However, 59% of citizens 62 and older voted, comprising 35% of the total votes cast, while only 36% of those younger than 62 voted, representing the other 65% of the voters.[52] (Voter data for the 2016 election cycle won't be available from the Census Bureau until later in 2017.)

Note: Social Security and Medicare were not issues on the ballot in the November 2014 election. But what if these issues are on the ballot? An even larger share of those over 62 will certainly vote. When it comes to these retirement and healthcare programs that are so critical to the financial well-being of seniors, party affiliation is irrelevant. Seniors will vote in a block for whoever is committed to sustaining the programs—better still if the politician proposes to enhance the programs. How would they treat a politician who takes a stand to cut their benefits?

The fact is, we will probably never know, because it won't happen. Politicians have learned over many decades that there is no win in proposing to cut Social Security or Medicare. This is not surprising. Social Security accounts for over 50% of household income for 61% of beneficiaries. For one-third of all retirees, Social Security provides over 90% of their household income.[53]

The Three-Legged Stool of Retirement

However, even these statistics understate the extent to which retirees rely on Social Security benefits. That's because they include the sizeable number of households in which a "retiree" continues to earn income while also collecting a benefit—in other words, they haven't really retired yet. When we take the earned income out of the mix the result is a more accurate picture of how important Social Security is to retirees once they have stopped working. Once the earned income stops, Social Security makes up a much higher proportion of total household income across the board.

In my view this is the most under-reported story concerning retirement. The myth prevalent among the public is that financial planning for retirement consists of a three-legged stool: Social Security benefits, pen-

---

52 Census data: *http://www.census.gov/data/tables/time-series/demo/voting-and-registration/p20-577.html Table 1*
53 *https://www.ssa.gov/policy/docs/chartbooks/fast_facts/2016/fast_facts16.pdf* Page 8

sion benefits, and income from savings (including retirement accounts like 401(k)s and IRAs). Take a look at the following table to see the reality of retirement finance.

Sources of Income Excluding Work Income For People Aged 65 and Older — Excluding Public Pensions	
Social Security (56%) and Gov't Transfers* (19%)	57%
Pensions/Savings (Including 401ks, IRAs etc.)	21%
Assets	16%
Other (Workers Comp, Alimony, Unemployment Ins. etc.)	6%
Total	100.0%
*Gov't Transfers include Veterans' Benefits and Supplemental Security Income, etc.	
Source: Author tabulation from Social Security Administration data[54]	

The dirty little secret is that once we stop working, Social Security is what we live on, making up over 57% of our income (for those of us who do not have a public pension from working in the public sector). But wait, it's even more extreme for most of us. If we further exclude the wealthiest 20% from this data, looking only at the bottom 80% (the vast majority of us), Social Security and government transfers[55] make up between two-thirds and 95% of our annual incomes in retirement.[56] Fewer and fewer of us receive pensions anymore; as for the rest of us, if we had to survive on only savings and assets our lives in retirement would be meager indeed.

In reality, the finances of the vast majority of seniors who no longer work consist essentially of a one-legged stool that stands almost entirely on Social Security. If you see yourself in this picture—if you don't have a huge amount of savings and retirement accounts or a pension—you should take heart in knowing that you are squarely in the same boat as about 80% of us. You are far from alone. (Once we recognize that Social Security is the single most important financial asset for most of us, the next step is to figure out how to get the most out of that asset—that's the subject of the second and third sections of this book.)

---

54 Social Security Administration, "Income of the Population 55 or Older, 2014", Pub No. 13-11871, April 2016, Tables 10.1 and 10.5
55 Mostly Supplemental Security Income (SSI), which is part of the Social Security program providing extra income to the very poorest seniors
56 Social Security Administration, "Income of the Population 55 or Older, 2014", Pub No. 13-11871, April 2016, Tables 10.1 and 10.5, author tabulation from data.

Live in Caribbean Belize for $60 a Day or Less
By Ann Kuffner, *InternationalLiving.com*

Lots of expats are already living their dream Caribbean lifestyle... Taking leisurely walks along the coast, cooled by the enticing Caribbean breeze...swimming and snorkeling in the living aquarium of the Caribbean Sea...feasting on fresh fruits, seafood and lobster...indulging in afternoon catnaps in a comfy hammock...meeting friends for a fresh catch lunch at a seaside café...

Here's the good news—this idyllic Caribbean lifestyle is still possible for those with a decent Social Security income—if they know where to settle, and how to cut corners...

Financially savvy expats are enjoying this enviable lifestyle on $60 a day, or less. Many expats choose to spend more... but plenty get by on less. It's a matter of making lifestyle choices that fit within your individual budget.

Belize has garnered significant tourism attention during the last few years, especially for the highly popular cayes. It is, of course, more costly to live in the most desirable regions frequented by tourists—the cayes and the Placencia Peninsula. (The cost of living on the Placencia Peninsula is now comparable to the cost of living on Ambergris Caye.) And yet there are expats who insist they have been living a comfortable, quality lifestyle in these popular regions, but on an affordable budget...

So let's explore the daily cost of living in a few of the popular regions of Belize where the majority of expats settle—Ambergris Caye, Corozal, Punta Gorda and San Ignacio...

Cost of Living on Ambergris Caye: $60 a Day

Ambergris Caye continues to rack up awards as one of the world's best islands to retire. This gorgeous Caribbean island is within easy reach of the spectacular World Heritage Mesoamerican Barrier Reef, with myriad options to explore its many splendors. Because it is an island, there is an "extra" cost for products shipped there. And tourism has driven up wages. And yet, retirees Judy and Dwayne Allen live comfortably on Ambergris Caye for less than $60 a day. Like many expats in Belize, they own their own home, so don't worry about the rental trends. The Allens are living a satisfying, comfortable lifestyle.

Cost of Living in Corozal: $42 a Day

On the mainland, the town of Corozal is a less expensive alternative. This expat haven, a 90-minute water taxi ride from Ambergris Caye, sits on the picturesque Bay of Corozal. You'll find an active, established expat community here. And quite a few of the expats living here subsist on their Social Security income. It's possible to do because the cost of living in this region starts at $42 a day for a couple. One of the advantages in this region is that expats can easily cross the border and stock up on inexpensive bulk items in Chetumal, Mexico, at familiar chain stores like Sam's Club.

Angi and John Eurton moved to Corozal over two years ago. Angi notes: "It's extremely cheap to live here. We spend far more than we need to simply because we can. You could easily spend less than $1,500 per month and live very well."

John Wiankowski is another expat who lives in Corozal full-time. He appreciates the inexpensive fresh produce, which is ripe and full of flavor. For just 50 cents he can buy eight oranges, four limes, or eight bananas; fresh fish fillets for $3.50/lb.; and local lobsters for $9/lb. He rented a one-bedroom apartment in Corozal for $450 a month before completing his new home.

Cost of Living in Punta Gorda and the Cayo: $42 a Day

Heading to the southern end of Belize, Punta Gorda is another charming small town on a bay. Penny Leonard owns a small home with a bay view. Her cost of living is $36 a day. For a couple renting a home in this area, they could get by on $42 a day.

For those who aren't yearning to live by the Caribbean Sea, another option is to head for the hills. For some expats, the Cayo region's rivers, ruins and jungles are more enticing than the beach and coastal towns on the Caribbean Sea. The cost of living in and around San Ignacio also starts around $42 a day.

Living on Your Social Security in Belize

Expats who depend mainly on their Social Security income to live in Belize tend to pay attention to the cost of "discretionary" items. They cut corners by buying mostly local products and brands, and eat more like the locals. For instance, a box of imported cereal runs $7. And imported potato chips are about $4.50 to $5 a bag. My husband and I prefer to buy fresh local tortillas and make our own, healthier corn chips. A pack of 20 fresh tortillas runs only $1 on Ambergris Caye. We cut up the tortillas, add some salt and seasonings, then pop them in the toaster oven. These low cost, healthy chips are perfect with homemade guacamole or the local salsa.

Another way to control costs is to buy or rent a home designed to take advantage of the Caribbean's cooling sea breezes. Most of our expat friends seldom use their air-conditioning units, saving hundreds of dollars each month on their electricity bill.

If you do decide to live on a caye, you can also cut costs by living near town and hoofing it, instead of buying a golf cart. Expats who live close to San Pedro Town save a bundle by getting around on their bike, or on foot. When they need to make a major shopping trip to town they opt for a taxi. Their overall transportation costs are negligible.

Another trick is to opt for water taxis instead of flights and buses whenever possible. On the mainland, bus fares are affordable, especially when compared to flying or renting a vehicle.

It's easy to control your entertainment budget in Belize. There are plenty of no cost entertainment options...live bands regularly jam on the beach—for free... There are many festivals, parades and performances—also for free... Enjoy parks with no entrance fees, walk on the beach, sit under a palapa at the end of a dock, swim in the Caribbean Sea, hike in a jungle... All are pleasant, free activities expats enjoy.

And there's no charge for the enriching companionship shared with new friends.

It's not just Baby Boomers who will Benefit from Social Security

Now that we understand the extent to which the majority of beneficiaries depend overwhelmingly on Social Security for their income, we can make the reasonable bet that this massive block of voters will not take kindly to any action (including no action) that would substantially diminish their benefits. Any politician who proposes otherwise is likely to run into a firestorm of opposition, opposition that is united around preventing such cuts and opposition that is motivated to vote accordingly.

Think about it: We arrive in the 2030s and it begins to look like the government is considering cutting benefits 20%-plus across the board to balance Social Security solely on the backs of current retirees. By that time there will be roughly 75 million beneficiaries.[57] The vast majority doesn't have the slack in their budgets to absorb such a pay cut without being forced to drastic choices among medicine, food, and shelter. Imagine mil-

---

57 *https://www.ssa.gov/OACT/TR/2016/* The 2016 OASDI Trustees Report, Table V.C4, page 132

lions and millions of these folks with their canes, walkers, and wheelchairs descending upon Washington, D.C., to let their representatives know exactly how they feel. Imagine the beating they would deliver to those politicians blocking a more judicious fix that spreads the pain far more broadly. As we have already seen, such a fix is well understood. Imagine those politicians quickly crumbling before the pressure... That last part is not hard to imagine at all!

Yet retirees aren't the only ones who want to preserve Social Security. The program also enjoys overwhelming support from younger voters, even those who are decades from starting their benefits (and even though most of these Gen Xers and Millennials don't believe the program will be there for them). Polls repeatedly show that over 70% of younger Americans would pay more in taxes to protect the program for current seniors as well as for themselves.[58]

Perhaps that's not so surprising: Today's beneficiaries are their parents and their grandparents. Basically, we work and pay so our parents and grandparents can live in a measure of dignity and financial security—and maybe so they won't need to come live with us! And the program is designed for each generation to provide for prior ones in a similar manner with a couple of neat twists: Each younger generation actually gets a much higher benefit (because this benefit is tied over time to the ever-increasing prevailing wage rate) out of the system when they retire! How cool is that?

Given such widespread support for Social Security across generations, there is only one realistic possibility for dealing with the looming short-fall: Fix the problem and return the program to a reasonable degree of fiscal stability. As we know now, there are many ways to accomplish this with minimal impact to current or future beneficiaries—"tweaks" to the program.

Would fixing Social Security (again) be so costly that it would damage the overall economy? As we saw earlier the impact of possible tax increases has been absorbed in the past without great impact. Still, can the overall

---

58 https://www.nasi.org/learn/social-security/public-opinions-social-security

economy afford it? The Social Security trustees provide a measurement for this as well: The program currently consumes about 5% of GDP and it would have to rise to about 6% to stabilize it.[59]

Where could we find that extra 1%? The simple answer is to grow the economy… However, we can also argue that there is already plenty of wealth in the economy to afford it. For example, it is well understood that the U.S. spends over 17% of GDP on healthcare—6% more than any of the other developed economies (though our healthcare outcomes are no better and in some cases worse…).[60] In other words, we essentially over-pay for healthcare by 6% of GDP. While it would be silly to suggest that we just take 1% out of healthcare—it doesn't work that way—the point is that we have an enormously wealthy economy, one in which we can apparently afford to waste about 6% of GDP on overpaying for healthcare without any extra benefit to show for it. When we cannot afford other programs that are dear to us, we will find a way to find the money and it probably won't harm the economy in a significant way.

As we near the end of our discussion of why it's a smart bet to assume that Social Security will be there for you in full, I want to leave all this history and facts and figures and return to the fairy tale we looked into earlier. You know, the one about the time long ago in a land far away where the leader claimed that Social Security is basically sound; it just needs to be tweaked. And the opposition leader, standing right there, didn't object. Isn't that essentially the argument we have been trying to make ever since about Social Security? Structurally sound? Needs to be tweaked?

As it turns out, once again we learn that the truth is stranger than fiction—or fairy tales, in this case. During the first presidential candidate debate preceding the 2012 election held on October 3, 2012, at the University of Denver in Colorado, the following verbatim exchange took place:

---

59 *https://www.ssa.gov/OACT/TR/2016/index.html* The 2016 OASDI Trustees Report, pp. 15-16.
60 *http://data.worldbank.org/indicator/SH.XPD.TOTL.ZS*

little ("tweaks") and gets a lot (long-term solvency) remain readily available for whenever the politicians decide to roll up their sleeves and do the hard work of compromise.

Key Takeaways

Why will the looming Social Security shortfall be fixed in a manner that ensures the long-term stability of the program without any significant benefit cuts to current or future beneficiaries? Two basic reasons:

1. The program as it exists is simply too popular with the public for politicians to alter it in any fundamental way.

2. Once enacted, the changes required to maintain the solvency in the long term (at least 50 more years) will have minimal impact on taxpayers individually and the $18 trillion U.S. economy overall.

As we saw in a moment of unusually blunt honesty, the two presidential candidates of 2012, President Obama and Governor Romney, acknowledged as much in their debate by agreeing: "Social Security is structurally sound. It's going to have to be tweaked."

The 2016 candidates, Donald Trump and Hillary Clinton hardly even alluded to the needed tweaks, emphasizing mostly their similar commitment to preserve the program as it is.

Does that sound like a crisis in the Social Security program? No.

Social Security will be there for us in full throughout our retirements. That's the smart bet. Plan accordingly.

CHAPTER 6

Social Security: Part of the *New Deal*, Still a Good Deal

It's an Insurance Program, not a Retirement Account

As a society we have a tendency to talk about the Social Security program like it's mainly a retirement fund…and a pretty lousy one at that, because sometimes it doesn't even pay out nearly what we paid into it.

Looking at the program as a bad investment is the wrong way to think about it, and here's why.

Social Security isn't an investment program; it's an insurance program. It provides benefits for you and possibly your spouse, children, and parents if you become disabled during your working years. It also provides benefits to your survivors when you pass away, whether during your working career or after you retire. Most important is the insurance it provides you after you retire if you live a long, long time: a monthly check, guaranteed by the U.S. Government, adjusted each year to keep up with inflation for as long as you live, which can be quite a long time. That's financial security. (In fact, for many of us Social Security turns out to be a pretty good investment after all. We'll look into just how long we are likely to live and how the benefits can add up later in the book.)

Do You Complain About Car Insurance?

If you start to consider how most insurance works, Social Security starts to look better and better. Start with car insurance, usually the first one we acquire as adults when we get our first car. You pay and pay, year in and year out, and hope you never need to use it. Why? Because it means you had an accident (or someone driving your car did), and that's never a good thing, right? If you do file a claim, you just know the insurance company is going to jack up your rates down the road so it can recoup what it paid you. You try to keep the premium down by going to a higher deductible and/or trying to avoid filing a claim at all by covering the repair/damages yourself. Your premium can go up even if you don't have a claim: Just get a moving violation or two and see what happens! Still, no responsible person would own a car without auto insurance; we purchase it to be sure there is enough money to cover any property damage and medical care that might arise out of a serious accident.

Now imagine a time down the road, perhaps after you have given up your car and your license. Maybe you feel lucky if you never had a claim and never got a penny out of your insurance, or anyone else's. After all, that means you were never involved in a serious accident of any kind. Everything worked out fine between you and your insurance company, right? Do you expect to get your money back? Of course not! Do you complain about what a rotten deal it was, paying in all those years and never getting a penny back? Of course not.

Now suppose you had been in an accident and suffered injuries that caused you to be so disabled you could not return to work. Your car insurance (or that of the party at fault) will cover the car repairs and hospitalization and perhaps some rehabilitation. Your insurance is unlikely to provide any compensation if you can no longer work. However, if you have worked long enough paying payroll taxes to qualify for Social Security benefits (as little as 18 months for a younger worker), you can potentially qualify for disability benefits. And the amount of your benefit can be as high as what you would have received at your Full Retirement Age (between 66 and 67 currently, depending on your birth year), as if you had continued working to that age paying into the system all the while. Furthermore, once you qualify for disability benefits, you can also qualify for Medicare after two years even if you are decades away from reaching age 65. That's a major insurance benefit.

How Can Homeowners Insurance Help You?

Or take homeowners insurance. Again, we hope we never have to file a claim, since that means there was a fire or a pipe burst, causing a flood or something similar. When we sell our homes we don't regret all the money we paid in premiums if we never filed a claim. We don't expect to start to get our money paid back to us. Instead, we chalk it up to good fortune that we never needed to use the insurance. (And if you are a renter, rest assured, you are paying for the insurance that the owner buys in your monthly rental payment.)

As with the auto insurance, if there was an incident—such as a serious fire—that caused damage and severe burns to you requiring hospitalization, your insurance would likely cover costs for repair and medical care, and you would be glad you had it. However, if your burns prevented you from returning to work for many years, or perhaps forever, your home insurance wouldn't help out. But Social Security would, with disability benefits and possible Medicare access.

In both of these disability cases, the Social Security benefits can even be broader. If you have the disability and have minor-aged children or your parents living with you, you can qualify for family benefits that can be as much as 180% of your Full Retirement Age benefit.

What if the auto accident or the house fire resulted in death? Don't expect much from your auto or home insurance, beyond any property damages and hospitalization. Yet Social Security survivor benefits can kick in for remaining family members and dependents.

How Social Security is Different from Other Insurance Programs

Yet what really differentiates Social Security insurance from auto and car and any other kind of insurance is that in the end, if you live to your claiming age, Social Security insurance starts to pay you back for as long as you live, even if you are paid far more than what you paid in originally.

Did I mention your payments are guaranteed by the federal government? And adjusted annually for inflation? I did? Well, it's worth repeating, because Social Security is really one heck of an insurance program when you consider the whole package.

Finally, most people receiving benefits won't pay any income tax on their benefits. Most states exclude Social Security from tax entirely. As part of the Social Security Amendments of 1983 and further rules changes in 1993, up to 85% of Social Security benefits are subject to federal income tax on a sliding scale as your income increases. In 2014 about half of beneficiaries found part or all of their benefits subject to income tax. Of 2014 benefits paid, 6.5% was paid back in taxes, mostly by those with higher incomes.[64] (We'll look at this with some examples later in the book and you will see that you can have quite a bit of income with Social Security yet still pay very little in tax. That's as it should be: After all, you already paid income tax on your Social Security taxes when you paid them into the system.)

In sum Social Security provides a host of insurance benefits to us, our families, and our survivors for bad things happening to us during our working years, covering disability and death. Unlike other insurance, around the time we stop paying for Social Security "insurance" we start to receive a benefit for the rest of our lives, adjusted each year for inflation and guaranteed by the federal government. No other insurance program can match that.

And as we have learned in Section I, this program will almost certainly be there for us in full, as it will likely be for our children and grandchildren.

How do we determine how to get the most out of the Social Security program based on our personal circumstances? We turn to this crucial question next in Section II.

---

64 *https://www.cbo.gov/publication/49948*

Key Takeaways

While our book focuses on retirement benefits for workers, their spouses, and survivors, Social Security offers far more: disability benefits for those unable to work, along with family benefits that can cover spouses, children, and dependent parents under a number of circumstances. While we can all hope we never encounter a need to collect on these kinds of benefits, we can still be comforted to know they are there for us in case of misfortune.

Retire in Las Tablas, Panama for $1,000 a Month

By Jessica Ramesch, *InternationalLiving.com*

Located on Panama's Pacific Coast, little Las Tablas is Panama at its best. This town of under 30,000 people lies on the Azuero Peninsula, a region renowned for everything from colorful Carnival celebrations to artisanal textiles, pottery, and leatherwork. Life in this region of Panama is good.

It is graced with more sunny days and less humidity than any other part of the country. And the cost of living is the lowest in Panama: Here, a couple can easily live on $1,000 a month, including rent, as expats Joyclyn and Armand Brodeur have found out.

Originally from St. Louis, the Brodeurs came to Las Tablas in August 2014 to test-drive their Panama retirement, so to speak. Armand, 66, and Joyclyn, 59, long yearned for a tropical, beach lifestyle. At the same time, they wanted to choose a place where it was possible to live on a Social Security check. "Las Tablas fits the bill," they say, citing the excellent infrastructure and affordable healthcare.

The Brodeurs chose Las Tablas so they could live well, without sacrificing the good things in life.

And they were amazed at the local supermarket prices...55 cents for a beer and $4 for a bottle of wine. Says Armand, "I treat myself to Clan MacGregor scotch at $9 a bottle, about the same as up north. Bacon is about $4 a pound, but it costs even more in St. Louis." Even so, they spend just $65 a week on groceries.

Utilities are also extremely inexpensive. Their first power bill was around $20 (no air conditioning). "Our water is included in our rent, and trash pickup is $18 a year," they say. Vonage internet phone service is $32 a month and allows for toll-free calls to the U.S. and other countries. Add to that another $30 to $40 a month for two cellphones (calls plus data) and $52 for bundled cable and internet.

The Brodeurs are most enthusiastic about the quality and affordability of the healthcare, however. Both have been to a local dentist and were impressed with the offices, equipment, and thorough manner. "She's the best dentist I ever had," says Joyclyn. "Armand went in for a broken tooth and paid just $15."

"I thought I heard wrong," he says. "She spent an hour and a half on me; it was like a minor surgery. And there was no pain. They are not stingy with the Novocain down here."

With more money in their pockets and no shortage of time on their hands, the two have been able to fully immerse themselves into the local way of life. At a recent festival in rural Panama, Joyclyn and Armand had one of their first brushes with Panama's colorful culture. "I saw a bull run, and it was fascinating," says Joyclyn. There were oxcarts painted in bright primary colors, local boys in traditional garb, and girls in richly embroidered *polleras*—Panama's much-admired national costume.

"They would pose and display their dresses," she says. "It was the best party I had ever seen. I even danced with an older local man. The music was playing and he was twirling me around," she says, smiling at the memory.

The people of Panama are another major plus for the Brodeurs. "The neighbors are very friendly and we are inundated regularly with gifts of wonderful Panamanian food," says Armand.

When they're not dancing and socializing, you can often find Armand and Joyclyn enjoying their home in Las Tablas. Says Armand, "The day starts with Panamanian coffee—usually on the front porch. We have a papaya tree in the backyard and have fresh papaya regularly for breakfast." It's a simple, effortless lifestyle though the nearby beaches do make it sound a bit glamorous.

In the Pedasí region, about 45 minutes away by car, are some of Panama's most pristine stretches of sand. And the fishing is legendary. But the ocean-loving Brodeurs don't have to go far to get their fix. The craggy shores of Uverito beach are mere minutes from the Las Tablas town square.

"Our anniversary was in December, and we spent it at Uverito," say the Brodeurs. Christmas Day and New Year's Day found them back again, enjoying the beach alongside many locals. "We lament to friends on Facebook about the gruelling 11-minute drive to the beach," Armand jokes.

Trips to Uverito aside, the Brodeurs do most of their traveling by foot, as many of the locals do. And all the walking has had an unintended effect. "We have dropped an incredible amount of weight," says Armand. "And we're not even eating as healthy as we ought to." Joyclyn says walking is also the best way to get the lay of the land. "I know where to go for a lot of things now...and with the hot weather, we don't eat as much. I've dropped a whole size," she adds.

Las Tablas is a far cry from Panama City. You'll find no skyscrapers here...in fact, structures more than two stories tall are rare. Condo living is more of an abstract concept here, as people tend to live in boxy, wide-terraced homes. In most cases, they are framed by greenery that runs right up to the road. Here and there is a *casa de quincha*, a country cottage made the old-fashioned, wattle-and-daub way, with clay and straw.

The town plaza is graced by a small, white, colonial church. Like most of Las Tablas, it is unassuming, though visitors who enter are met with the soft glow of the ornate gold altar, a relic from Panama's earliest colonial days.

A short walk from the main plaza, the Brodeurs have rented a small home for $200 a month. They paid $600 for a slightly upscale apartment during their first month in Las Tablas. It was ready to move into and in a central location, so it worked while they were getting settled. Soon, however, they were ready to try a local-style home. They just did a bit of networking— and used the few words of Spanish they've learned since their arrival. It paid off. An expat introduced them to a local homeowner and the next thing they knew, they were signing a new rental agreement.

These days, the Brodeurs say they have many more friends—both Panamanian and expat—than they did "back up north." Life is more social and more fun. As Las Tablas is at the nation's center, they can travel anywhere with ease. They recently visited Panama City—it's about four hours by car due east. The western province of Chiriquí is similarly close, so they're planning a trip to the highland towns of Boquete and Volcán Barú in the near future.

Will the Brodeurs stay in Las Tablas? Who knows—they are still exploring the country, and they're keeping an open mind. A few months into their "test drive," however, they're already quite certain that Panama is right for them. "I wanted access to the ocean, friendly people, and palms...and I got it all," says Joyclyn. "It would not break our hearts to live in Las Tablas for the balance of our days," says Armand.

benefits at that same age? Keep in mind that the money to make this purchase would need to come out of an after-tax savings account.

Let's look at an example. Suppose we reach Full Retirement Age this year (66 in 2017) and have average annual career earnings in 2017 dollars of around $60,000. We would qualify for a benefit of roughly $2,000 a month. What would we have to pay to purchase an equivalent amount of benefit that adjusts each year for inflation from an insurance company?

The answer is around $520,000 for a male and $560,000 for a female.[66] (Why would women need to pay more for the same benefit amounts? Recall that women tend to live longer than men; consequently they would need to pay extra for the additional years of life during which the insurance company issuing the annuity would expect to still be paying.) If such a male and female are married, their combined benefit value is around $1,080,000. Remember, the money to purchase this stream of lifetime payments would have to come from after-tax savings. Few couples have savings greater than this amount; few have home equity greater than this amount. And $60,000 in average lifetime career earnings is solid, though not unusually high.

Suppose the wife in this couple has little or no work record. Then she is eligible to receive half of what he is eligible to receive if he claims at age 66. Half of $2,000 is $1,000, and they would need about $280,000 additional (that's half of the $560,000 it would cost a female to purchase the $2,000 annuity at 66). In other words, the couple would need about $520,000 + $280,000 = $800,000 in savings to purchase a combined monthly benefit of $3,000 at age 66 from an insurance company as an annuity.

How Social Security is Our Single Most Valuable Asset

Of course, we do not have the choice to take our Social Security benefits as a lump sum. The purpose of this exercise is to translate our likely benefit streams into amounts of equivalent savings so we can more

---

66 Based on quotes for annuities with an annual CPI adjustment accessed at *www.immediateannuities.com* by author in February 2017

readily compare them to our other financial assets such as savings or the equity in our homes.

We have one more important question to consider in this exercise: How does the cost of the annuity change if we claim the benefit earlier or later? Let's go back to the first case, in which both husband and wife qualify for a work-based benefit of $2,000 at Full Retirement Age of 66. The various annuity prices at 62, 66, and 70 are laid out in the table below.

Cost to Purchase an Inflation Protected Annuity Equal to Social Security Benefits as Various Claim Ages[67]			
	Male	Female	Combined
Claim at Age 62			
Monthly Benefit	$1,500	$1,500	$3,000
Equivalent Annuity Cost	$440,000	$470,000	$910,000
Claim at Age 66			
Monthly Benefit	$2,000	$2,000	$4,000
Equivalent Annuity Cost	$520,000	$560,000	$1,080,000
Claim at Age 70			
Monthly Benefit	$2,640	$2,640	$5,280
Equivalent Annuity Cost	$590,000	$640,000	$1,230,000

Note that the cost of purchasing the annuities increases substantially the longer we wait to claim. This is what the marketplace is telling us: Our age 70 combined benefits (using the case in the table) would cost us $150,000 to $170,000 more than our age 62 benefits. That's right: Insurance companies would charge us considerably more for the higher claim amounts at age 70, even though they would expect to pay those amounts for eight fewer years.

---

67 Ibid.

Conclusion: Our Social Security benefits are precious, the single most valuable financial asset under our control for nearly all of us. (And if you are among the successful few who have a greater financial asset, you are probably still surprised to learn just how valuable your Social Security benefits are in comparison.) What do we do with valuable financial assets? We look after them to get the most we can out of them. For retirement accounts and other savings that means managing our portfolios (or hiring someone to do that for us). For our homes that means maintaining the building and property to maximize the eventual sale value.

We also have to manage our Social Security, although the process is different from managing our savings and our homes. Our primary purpose as we continue through this book is to become well prepared to successfully manage our benefits. Hey, it beats going out and cleaning the gutters before the next rains or preparing for another planning session with our brokers to manage our investments! And the great news is that once we develop a custom claiming strategy that best meets our needs and circumstances, it's pretty much set-it-and-forget-it from then on out.

Happier, Healthier, and Wealthier in Salinas, Ecuador

By Denver Gray, *InternationalLiving.com*

For almost three years now, I've been living with my wife in a beautiful beachfront condo on the Pacific Ocean. That sentence alone might lead you to believe we live an expensive lifestyle. But not so. Thanks to the savings we made in moving our lives to Salinas, I have been able to retire this year at the ripe old age of 57. Here, I am happier, healthier, wealthier, and enjoying life to the fullest.

Just four years ago, I would not have believed it possible. In spite of a family income of six figures, we were still not able to put much toward retirement. We were living in a great waterfront condo in Maryland, but at a cost. Our monthly expenses were over $6,000. Our HOA fees alone were almost $900. On top of that, property taxes were about $5,000 a year. We were happy living there, but I was resigned to working until I was 65, at least.

Then we started looking into Ecuador as an option. My wife had already retired from real estate, and my job was portable. So after some due diligence, we decided to go see for ourselves.

The rest, as they say, is history. We fell in love with the seaside resort town of Salinas, and purchased a 2,000-square-foot beachfront condo in a modern building. We sold the place in Maryland and bought a smaller home for cash (no mortgage) to store some of our furniture and as Plan B, just in case Ecuador was not all we hoped it would be.

What a difference it has made in our lives. Our monthly expenses dropped from more than $6,000 to less than $2,000. Our property taxes went from $5,000 a year to an almost laughable $270. HOA fees are $169 instead of $900. We sold our cars when we moved, and with cheap buses and cabs available in our new home, and most things in walking distance anyway, we don't need the expense of a car or car insurance anymore. I love to cook, and the fresh produce, seafood, and meat here makes it even more fun. But when we do feel the urge to dine out, it costs us less than $20 for the two of us, instead of $50 or more.

Although we started living more cheaply, we also started living better. The great climate, fresh air, fresh food, and walking two to six miles a day have greatly improved our health.

Instead of spending my days dealing with other people's network problems, I can now spend time doing the things

I enjoy. I can take time to write more, spend more time studying Spanish, practice playing the musical instruments we brought with us, and spend quality time with my wife and family. We look forward to exploring Ecuador, and possibly even applying for citizenship. With Ecuador as such an inexpensive base, we will have time, health, and opportunity now to travel to other places around South America and the world.

Are Our Future Benefits the Best Asset in Our Financial Portfolios?

Maybe.

Let's turn this conversation around for a moment and consider what happens each time we postpone taking our benefits for a year. Suppose our Full Retirement Age benefit is $2,000 (as in the case above). If we defer taking it for a year, we leave $24,000 ($2,000 x 12 months) on the table for that year. In exchange—and assuming we start our benefits the next year—we get an 8% increase in our benefits thereafter, an added $160 a month, $1,920 a year, increased annually for inflation for life. Put another way, it's as if at age 66 we pay an insurance company $24,000 and they issue an inflation-protected annuity that pays us $1,920 each year for the rest of our lives. In simplest terms, the annuity pays 8%, adjusted for inflation, for life.

If we look at the market for inflation protected annuities it turns out that we cannot find a comparable product that pays anywhere near 8%—never mind that the Social Security product is guaranteed by the government. Indeed, such products pay within the range of 3.8% (female at 62) to 5.4% (Male at 70)[68] (a little higher for men at a given age, a little lower for women at that same age—again, because women live longer). Anyone considering an annuity of any kind should first "invest" this

---

68 Based on quotes obtained by the author in February 2017 from *www.immediateannuities.com*

money in postponing making a claim for Social Security because they will be nearly doubling their rate of return compared to what an insurance company will pay. Any investment advisor who is honest will be hard pressed to find an investment product of comparable risk that pays such a high guaranteed rate of return.

Key Takeaways

To purchase an annuity from an insurance company that would pay us an amount equal to our Social Security benefits—adjusted each year for the rest of our lives—would cost $250,000 to $750,000-plus for an individual. A married couple's benefits are worth $500,000 to well over $1 million. That's the largest financial asset that 90% of us own—greater than our savings and retirement accounts or the net equity in our homes. Isn't it worth investing the time to get educated about what is probably our most valuable asset?

CHAPTER 8
When to Start Benefits? Don't Look to the SSA for Help

Warning! The Social Security Administration (SSA) will mislead you...

We are committed to uncovering what we need to know in order to get the most out of our Social Security benefits. We assert—and soon we will demonstrate—that wise management of our claiming strategy will usually generate tens of thousands of additional dollars in cumulative lifetime benefits for singles and commonly $100,000—even hundreds of thousands—for married couples. Indeed, knowing how best to "play" Social Security can give us the retirement lifestyles we deserve.

You would think that the Social Security Administration (SSA) would be the place to go to find reliable advice on how to get the most from our benefits and specifically, to get the answer to this question: "What is the best age to sign up for my benefits?" You would be wrong. The administration's highly rated website[69] is a place where you can spend many hours and more yet not find a straightforward answer to this crucial question.

Let's Search for Advice...

Still, if we sift through the tea leaves at the SSA website we can extract critically valuable information. To start, we go to *www.ssa.gov*, where we find a handy search box on the upper right of each page that searches only within their website. Enter a question like "Best age to start benefits?" or

---

69 *https://gcn.com/articles/2015/02/19/egov-satisfaction-survey.aspx*

"When should I collect benefits?" or "How do I decide between age 62 or 70 or another age?"

At the top of the list of responses is a document titled "When to Start Receiving Retirement Benefits."[70] (This source is also referenced in the statements that are periodically sent out to prospective beneficiaries.) Sounds promising. Let's read on:

> At Social Security, we're often asked, "What is the best age to start receiving retirement benefits?"

Exactly the question we have in mind! Bingo! Right? And the document is only two pages, so the answer must be close at hand. Ready? Have a look at their response to the question:

> Would it be better for you to begin receiving benefits early with a smaller monthly amount or to wait for a larger monthly payment later that you may not receive as long? The answer is personal and depends on several factors, such as your current cash needs, your current health, and family longevity. Also, consider if you plan to work in retirement or if you have other retirement income sources. You must also study your future financial needs and obligations and, of course, calculate your future Social Security benefit. **We hope you will weigh all the facts carefully** *[emphasis added]* and consider your own circumstances before making the important decision about when to begin receiving Social Security benefits...

Wait! That doesn't tell us anything. "Weigh all the facts carefully"? That's why we went to the SSA website, to get some guidance on *how* to "weigh all the facts." Thanks for nothing...

OK, at least they do acknowledge elsewhere in the document that "there's no one best age for everyone and, ultimately, it's your choice. You should make an informed decision about when to apply for benefits based on your individual and family circumstances."

---

70 *www.ssa.gov/pubs/EN-05-10147.pdf*

The bottom line is we won't get useful advice on figuring out the best age for us to start our benefits (beyond what we saw above) on the SSA website, nor will we get it by calling them or going to an appointment in one of their field offices. As we will discover by the end of this section, how and when we start our benefits is a complicated matter to consider carefully. Unfortunately, the agency does not have the staff and the time to engage in these kinds of complex consultations.

A Review of the Website

The SSA was subject to the effects of budget sequestration pursuant to the Budget Control Act of 2011. As a consequence, reductions in hiring and field office hours were applied beginning in 2013. This corresponds to a period when initial claims were rising steadily with the aging baby boomer population. The impact of the cuts was reflected in the wait times for those trying to call the agency, which reached a peak of just over 22 minutes in 2014.

The agency is quickly adopting new technologies to improve service with fewer people. They introduced automated callback technology, which reduced the call waiting time to around 12 minutes in 2015.[71] More significantly for budget purposes the SSA has developed a state-of-the-art website where they drive beneficiaries aggressively with the result that over 50% of claim applications were processed online in 2014.[72] Their web services are well designed:

> Our websites continue to shine; we have five of the seven top-rated government websites, and two of our websites are rated higher than the top private-sector sites.[73]

The entire Social Security Administration consumes just 1.3% of payouts to beneficiaries;[74] as taxpayers we can justly applaud their relative efficiency. Unfortunately, the technologies that permit the SSA to operate on limited finances don't lend themselves to providing the quality and depth of advice we need regarding when to start benefits. In fact, agents are trained to sign us up at first contact if possible:

---

71 *https://www.ssa.gov/budget/FY16Files/2016BO.pdf* 2016 SSA Fiscal Year Budget, page 10
72 Ibid., page 2
73 Ibid., page 7
74 Ibid., page 8

Whenever a potential claimant visits a FO [field office] and wishes to file, make every effort to complete an application and obtain the claimant's signature.[75]

Nothing will be found in that training guideline about offering advice and guidance. Instead, the primary goal is to sign us up at the first opportunity so they don't have to take time dealing with us again later. Efficient? Yes. Helpful in assisting us in getting the most out of our benefits? No.

Where We Can Find a Fundamental Starting Point

While we won't get the answer from the SSA to our question about when is the best time to claim our benefits, we can get a fundamental starting point for our effort to determine the best age to begin benefits from their website. Up until November 2016, you could find the following nugget buried in the two-pager we have been examining:

If you live to the average life expectancy for someone your age, *you will receive about the same amount in lifetime benefits no matter whether you choose to start receiving benefits at age 62, Full Retirement Age, age 70, or any age in between*. [Emphasis added]

(As I was updating this book for the 2017 edition, I was surprised to discover that this statement was removed late last year. This has been part of this publication since as early as 2009 when it was first published. As we look further into it, it will be clearer why they finally took it out; we will be left with the question as to why it took SSA so long.)

We need to unpack this statement carefully, because it is at once dangerously misleading and apparently entirely wrong. Let's look at how this can be.

I don't know about you, but the first several times I read the SSA's statement I drew this conclusion: If I'll get about the same amount in lifetime benefits regardless of when I start, I might as well start at 62; that way, if I happen to die before I turn 70, at least I got something out of the program, right?

---

75 Get What's Yours: The Secrets to Maxing Out Your Social Security, Laurence J. Kotlikoff, Philip Moeller, and Paul Solman, Simon & Schuster, 2015, page 59

Wrong!

How is the SSA's Answer Misleading us?

Here's the misleading part of their statement: "If you live to the average life expectancy for someone your age…"

Here's why that statement is misleading: In the context of this document, "someone your age" is 62 years old, the earliest age at which someone can start to collect retirement benefits. Not to go all math-y at this point (never mind morbid-y), but the average is made up of all the ages at which all the people who are 62 on any given day (about 10,000) happen to pass away. Some will pass away soon and others not for months, years, even decades. Surely some will still be alive past age 102, 40 years later. These 10,000 souls don't pass away all at the same time or even within a couple of years of one another. Instead, their deaths are spread out over three to four decades for the most part. The "average" is, say, one year that can be determined by adding up all those ages when folks pass away and dividing by the number in the group—in this case, 10,000. Even if we consider the "average life expectancy" to be "give or take a year or two," the fact is that over 80% of folks will pass away either before that four- to five-year window or after it, even well after it. (Never mind that most of those 20% who do happen to live to around the average life expectancy—they don't know who they are yet.)

In sum, relatively few people will live to the "average life expectancy" for someone who is 62, so the statement doesn't apply to them. Maybe it would have been more accurate if the following were added after that particular statement:

> On the other hand, if you are among the vast majority who will not live to the average life expectancy for someone your age, you will receive more or less—and in many cases substantially more or less—depending on the particular age at which you choose to start receiving benefits.

(Later in this section we will take a much closer look at exactly how much more or less we might collect over our lifetimes depending on when we start our claims.)

How the SSA Contradicts Itself

It is bad enough that this SSA statement misleads the vast majority of us to believe that it doesn't matter much when we start our benefits. However, it's worse: It turns out the SSA statement doesn't even appear to be true for those who "live to the average life expectancy," either. For the proof of why this is so, we turn to—get ready for it—the Social Security Administration.

The SSA by law gets informed when each of us is born and when we die. That data provides an awesome database for determining life expectancy by sex for various ages. In fact, you can look up your life expectancy based on your current age at this link on the SSA website: *https://www.socialsecurity.gov/oact/population/longevity.html.*

If we enter the birth year as if someone is 62 today we quickly see that the average life expectancy for a male is 83 and 8 months (83.7), for a female 86 and 4 months (86.3). (That's right, on average women tend to live over two-and-a-half years longer than men. That is a major factor to consider when planning a claiming strategy for married couples, as we will see later.)

Getting back to our basic question about living to the average life expectancy, we can now answer whether the Social Security Administration's statement that we will get about the same amount in cumulative benefits either way is true...or not.

Rich and Kathy: How Much Will They Make?

Consider two 62-year-olds: Rich and Kathy. Coincidentally, each is eligible to the same benefit at Full Retirement Age—66 for them—in the amount of $2,000 a month. (As noted earlier, this is roughly the benefit amount for someone who earned around $60,000 a year in 2017 dollars on average throughout their working career.) If each claims early, at 62, the monthly amount is reduced 25% to $1,500. Wait to age 70 and the amount increases 32% to $2,640 (plus all the inflation that happens between ages 62 and 70). Clearly it pays to wait if one wants that higher monthly benefit—but is it worth it over the long term?

If it's true as the SSA has asserted for years that "If you live to the average life expectancy for someone your age, you will receive about the same amount in lifetime benefits no matter whether you choose to start receiving benefits at age 62, full retirement age, age 70 or any age in between…" then it shouldn't matter much when Rich or Kathy start out —assuming each lives to their average life expectancy. Well, let's take a look at how that works out.

As noted above, Rich's average life expectancy is 83 and 8 months. If he starts collecting $1,500 a month at age 62, he will have collected $390,600 by the time he reaches that age. If instead Rich claims at 70 then he has collected $434,000 when he reaches 83 and 8 months. That's a bit over $43,000 more collected. That's real money. Definitely not chump change.

This result is illustrated in the chart below:

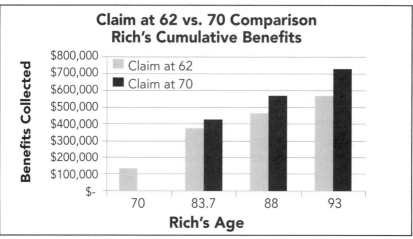

This chart shows what Rich has collected cumulatively when he reaches various ages. For instance, at age 70 he has already received $144,000 under the claim-at-62 strategy. If he just claimed at 70, he hasn't received anything yet! By the time he is 83.7 years old, his average life expectancy, we can see that he is about $43,000 ahead if he claimed at 70; at 88, the age that one in four men will live to, he is $102,000 ahead, and at 93, the age one in 10 men will live to, Rich is $171,000 ahead.

Now let's look at Kathy. Her average life expectancy at age 62 is age 86 and four months. If she starts her benefit at 62, that adds up to $437,400. Wait to claim at age 70 and she will have collected $516,380—nearly $79,000 more than the claim-at-62 strategy. That is most definitely not chump change. The chart below is comparable to the one for Rich:

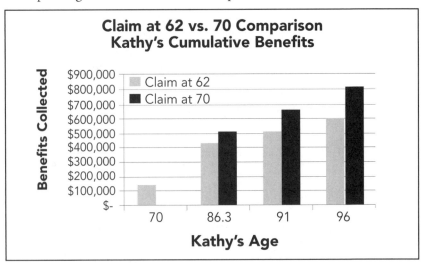

Her life expectancy is greater than Rich. This is clearly reflected in the chart where her average life expectancy of 86.3 years shows her nearly $79,000 ahead claiming at 70 versus 62. If she lives to the age that one in four women live to, 91, she is $143,000 ahead; at the age one in 10 women live to, 96, she is about $212,000 ahead. That's all in today's constant 2017 dollars.

In either case, male or female, according to the simple math, Rich and Kathy are tens of thousands of dollars ahead by waiting to claim at age 70 versus age 62—if they merely live to their average life expectancy.

Why do the numbers work out this way? Once they reach age 70 they are collecting $1,140 more each month, $13,680 more per year, compared with claiming at age 62. That extra money each month adds up quickly and catches up for the money that was not collected between 62 and 70 at the lower, age-62 benefit amount. In fact, when they reach 80 and six months of age they have collected the same amount whether they start at 62 or 70. That's three years and two months before Rich's average life expectancy and five years and ten months before Kathy's average life expectancy. Rich and Kathy are already ahead if they just live to just over age 80, well before their average life expectancy.

Let's summarize. Notwithstanding what the SSA declared on its website for many years up until just a few months ago, in fact if you are 62 and you wait to claim at 70 instead of 62 and you live to your average life expectancy, you will be considerably better off if you are male. And if you are female you will be enough ahead for it to be a no-brainer to wait. That's not what the SSA website would have had you think, yet it is exactly what their life expectancy numbers prove. While we should be heartened that SSA decided to remove this statement recently, we are left to wonder for the millions who may have been misled over the years and chosen a costly and inferior claiming strategy as a consequence.

Insurance Against Living Too Long...

We've been considering the question "How long will we live?" We've learned that this is a tricky question that takes on slightly different shading when we consider it in the context of Social Security. The better question is "How long *might* we live?" Answer: We might live a very long time, long past our assumed "expire by" dates. Way over half of the people who live to age 62 will make it to age 80. If there is a decent chance that we could be among them, finding a way to wait to claim until age 70 is well worth it and can pay off in tens of thousands, even hundreds of thousands, of dollars in extra income if we happen to live quite a long time. That's what you call excellent insurance against living a long life.

I've spoken at quite a few events before thousands of people, mostly baby boomers. No one who claimed early (and that's almost everyone) and has reached 70—when they are too old to do anything about their claiming choices—has ever come up to me to say they are glad they claimed early. On the contrary, to a person they wish they had known what they learned at the presentation before they filed because they believe they would have changed their claiming strategy.

What does this tell us? First, these folks by inference think they could have made it to a later claiming age somehow, so an unavoidable need for money at age 62 was not an excuse for them. Second, hindsight is 20-20: Those of us who have not yet claimed need to learn from the hard-earned lessons of those who claimed before us and use their wisdom to find the resolve to wait to claim later. We know it is isn't easy: Uncle Sam dangles that check out in front of our faces after a lifetime of work and it's exceedingly difficult to resist the temptation to grab it and run, even when we are convinced that the checks will keep coming in the future. That's just simple human nature. We need to resist this temptation in almost all cases. That is the most valuable message we will weave into this section on basic claiming strategy.

With this information and background at hand we can now turn to the matter of how to tailor a Social Security claiming strategy that will best serve each of us based on our particular circumstances.

What About Discounting? Net Present Value?

Financial wonks read on...

Many will say at this point, "Wait a minute! You are not allowing for discounting those dollars collected in the future beginning at age 70 compared with dollars beginning at age 62. You need to apply a discount factor..."

Short answer: No, we don't.

Why?

First and foremost, Social Security benefits are adjusted each year for inflation, so that eliminates one major component from the discount factor. Second, the remainder of the discount factor is tied primarily to the risk associated with future cash flows. The risk associated with future cash flows that are guaranteed by the U.S. government—that's essentially what Social Security benefits are—approaches zero. We can see this in the return on the Treasury's Inflation Protected Securities (TIPS). These are bonds for which the return is adjusted to cover any inflation, the "Inflation Protected" part. Currently these yield slightly under 1% on maturities greater than 10 years out. (Source: *www.treasury.gov/resource-center/data-chart-center/interest-rates/Pages/TextView.aspx?data=realyield accessed 02/09/17.*) Applying such a discount rate to future Social Security benefits has a non-substantial impact on the comparisons of cumulative benefits used throughout this book.

In addition, the "return" on Social Security benefits doesn't have a fixed maturity. It keeps paying no matter how long you live, so one should add some value for the possibility of a higher benefit possibly paid over more and more years. That's an option with significant, if indeterminate, value. Finally, this is the method generally recognized among those who provide Social Security benefit advice and consultations professionally.

Key Takeaways

Contrary to what the Social Security Administration says on its website, if we live to our average life expectancies once we reach age 62, we will be many tens of thousands of dollars ahead if we wait to claim our benefits at age 70 instead of age 62. And as we live longer past this point—as so many of us will—the extra dollars for claiming later keep piling up: Claiming at 70 is the best insurance against living a long life.

Sail the World on Your Social Security

By Amanda Walkins, *InternationalLiving.com*

Ann and Lew Tucker, from outside Albany, New York, now invite everyone into their brand-new home on the Caribbean island of Roatán, Honduras. From here they can relax on the upstairs patio and watch the boats float by, admiring the sunset over the Caribbean. Meanwhile, the gorgeous scent of orchids wafts up from the garden below.

The place they now call home is a Cape Cod-style cottage on the hillside of a popular neighborhood in West Bay. But this is a relatively recent development. For nearly two decades, they've been sailing around the world together.

Years ago, they discovered that a sailing retirement was a lot easier (and cheaper) than they ever could have realized. And they didn't need a vast amount of knowledge to get started.

"The boat is in a marina right now," Ann, 75, says. "We decided to start spending part of our time on land; as we get older, it's getting a little hard now to be on the boat year-round. But this summer we finally finished our circumnavigation!"

Named *Serannity*, their boat is a 48-foot Camper-Nicholson ketch and has been "home" for nearly their entire retirement. After getting married in 1985 and joining their families together, Ann and Lew (now 80), raised their five combined children, and the nest was empty as retirement neared.

"We owned a sailboat that we used in Lake Ontario occasionally, but that was really our only experience sailing until the early 1990s," says Ann. "That's when we took a trip on our boat down the St. Lawrence River. We learned more about sailing as we went. Lew just wanted to keep going, so we started making plans. By 1996, we were both retired, so we sold our home outside of Albany."

Aged 56 and 61, respectively, when they retired and set sail, Ann had spent her career as a special education teacher and Lew had been in construction. They used their retirement savings and the money from selling their home to fund their travels by sea.

With no monthly payments on rent or a mortgage, no utility payments, and very little temptation to eat at fancy restaurants when they're in the middle of the ocean, Ann and Lew's cost of living is incredibly low.

"We buy SIM cards in every country we stay in, and a modem if it still reaches offshore," says Ann. "It's easy to keep in touch, and those costs are so low everywhere in the world."

Their cost of living is so low, they can spend more on visiting new places and traveling all over the world. They can afford to fly from wherever they are to visit their children and grandchildren back home in the U.S. "We flew back from French Polynesia for a wedding, and another time from Australia for a visit," Ann says.

"When we first set sail we tracked every single expense on a spreadsheet," Lew continues. "Back then, we were spending about $15,000 to $20,000 per year. It's definitely possible to sail on Social Security."

The intrepid couple has visited many countries over the course of their adventure. Sometimes they moor off the coast and take daytrips to different areas; other times they rent a home for a few months to further explore a country. "For $200 per month, we rented a three-bedroom house with another cruising couple in Satun, Thailand," says Lew.

"We spent that time fixing the boat and enjoying some really low-cost living.

Ask them about their favorite country and they'll look at each other and chuckle. "There are so many," Lew says. They spent last year cruising through Belgium, Germany, the Netherlands, Denmark, Norway, and England. The year before, they sailed from South Africa to the U.K., leaving their boat in the Netherlands for the winter while they headed home to visit their grandkids. Another trip took them from the Galapagos Islands all the way to French Polynesia, the longest single passage they've done: 3,000 miles.

Ann and Lew have spent their retirement seeing the world on their own terms and on their own time.

CHAPTER 9
Social Security Basics
That May Apply to You

In the last chapter we looked at the simplest case for a work-based claim to illustrate clearly why, male or female, it is wise for nearly all of us to wait to claim at age 70 if at all possible. However, most of us are not solely workers and some of us aren't workers at all (we are not eligible for benefits under a work record). We can also be spouses, widows/widowers, and divorcees, and these circumstances can qualify us for other benefits. Sometimes we are a combination of these that may change over time: We start as a single with a work record, then get married, opening up the possibility of spouse benefits, and eventually one of us dies and survivor benefits come into play. (Reminder: There are also family benefits for minor and disabled children and dependent parents. These less-common benefits are not covered in this book. Get professional advice if you think these might apply to you.)

In this chapter we are going to run through a number of useful rules that determine when you might qualify for benefits and the amount you will be eligible to receive at any given point in time. We will ignore many other rules that are not necessary to developing a sound benefit claiming strategy. As we said before: If you want to learn to drive a car, there are basic rules you need to learn. However, you do not need to know much at all about what makes the car work, right? That would be a huge waste of time for most people. Most people never need to know what goes on under the hood and will still get every bit of benefit out of having a driver's license as the auto mechanic does.

I mention all this because Social Security is a hot mess when you look under the hood. If that fascinates you, there are a host of other books that wade into all the gory details. However, learning what goes on under the hood can suck up a lot of time without helping us get the most out of our benefits, so we won't spend our time on it here. My goal in writing this guide is to help you realize that you can use Social Security to your advantage—and by doing so lead a retirement even more comfortable than you may have thought possible.

That said, we will cover a number of common situations and circumstances, some of which may apply to you and some of which may not. You need to decide what applies; you can ignore the rest. (Unless, of course, it applies to your spouse, in which case you probably want to take note.)

Jargon We Need to Understand (as Little as Possible…)

The SSA uses a mind-bending, jargon-filled vocabulary. Unless we speak the language, it can be quite confusing. We will try to introduce only the minimum necessary to successfully navigate our way to finding a claiming strategy that's best for us.

Let's start with "eligibility": We are either eligible for a certain type of benefit or we aren't. For instance, in order to receive retirement benefits based on our work record (the Social Security taxes that we and our employer(s) paid into the system during our working career), we need to have a minimum amount of earnings per quarter ($1,300 in 2017—that's not much) during 40 calendar quarters (10 years), and we have to be at least 62 years old. (We may qualify for Disability Insurance benefits at a younger age; disability is a complex and specialized subject that we do not cover in this book. But it's comforting to know that these benefits are available to us should we need them.)

SSA Speak

Wondering what a Social Security rule reads like? Consider the following partial rule from Section 2 of the following policy. At times we may be simultaneously eligible for more than one benefit: This policy addresses how to determine which one. (Source: *https://secure.ssa.gov/apps10/poms.nsf/lnx/0300615170*)

RS 00615.170 Simultaneous Entitlement of a Widow(er) to Spouse's Benefits and RIB/DIB

2. Widow(er), Spouse and RIB/DIB

If the RIB/DIB exceeds the spouse's OB, the spouse's benefit is **stopped and the RIB/DIB is paid. If the RIB/DIB PIA is more than the spouse's OB, the spouse benefit is terminated. If the RIB/DIB PIA is less than the spouse's OB but for some reason the RIB/DIB benefit is higher than the spouse benefit, the spouse benefit is suspended and the spouse will be technically entitled.**

Note: Claimant has to be 62 or older to qualify for triple entitlement as D/W-B-HA. See SM 00820.100 and SM 00848.850 for triple entitlement computations.

Want to read more? Nah, we don't either…

We can be eligible for more than one benefit, in which case we generally receive an amount equal to the greater of the benefits for which we are aligible. We can be eligible for one benefit at one age and another (possibly greater) benefit at a later age. It is important to be aware of all the benefits to which we are or might become eligible because we won't always be granted the higher of the available benefits without first notifying the SSA; and if we don't notify them in a timely manner, we could end up forfeiting some or all of those benefits! We'll look at some examples later.

Next jargon item: "Full Retirement Age" (also referred to at times by the SSA as "Normal Retirement Age." Why both ways? No clue...). We will often refer to this as "FRA," so please try to remember this one. FRA is the base reference age from which our benefits are calculated. That is, when we claim early, our benefits are reduced from this age; when we claim later, our benefits are increased (called "Deferred Retirement Credits").

At the start of the Social Security program the FRA was set at age 65. However, as we noted in Section I the FRA was set to gradually rise to 67 pursuant to the Social Security Amendments (Public Law 98-21) of 1983, based on the rationale that people are living longer. Your FRA, therefore, depends on the year you were born, and you can find it in the table below:

Year of Birth	Full Retirement Age (FRA)
1946* - 1954	66
1955	66 and two months
1956	66 and four months
1957	66 and six months
1958	66 and eight months
1959	66 and 10 months
1960 and later	67
*If you were born before 1946 you are over 70 and should be already collecting benefits	

Types of Retirement Benefits You May Need to Understand

Here are the types of benefits we focus on in this book:

➢ **Work-Based Benefits:** You work and (currently) 6.2% of your income is paid to the SSA; in addition, your employer contributes a matching amount, another 6.2%. (If you are self-employed you pay both the employee and employer portion.) If you earn above a certain amount each year—$127,200 in 2017—you and your employer don't pay any more tax to the SSA for that calendar year. As noted above, once you have paid taxes in the minimum amounts for 10 years (40 calendar quarters—they do not need to be consecutive), you will become eligible to begin receiving a retirement benefit when you turn 62 based on those taxes you and your employer(s) contributed while you worked. (This is the kind of benefit we considered in our last chapter when looking at life expectancy and the decision whether to claim at 62 versus 70.)

Of course, most of us have paid in for far more than 10 years by the time we reach age 62. The SSA takes all your earnings on which you paid Social Security taxes into account in determining the amount of your benefit. While the exact methodology used in this calculation isn't worth your time to learn about, know that your benefit is paid on the 35 years during which you had the highest earnings. (A formula adjusts past earnings for inflation as well as for lower Social Security tax rates that applied before 1990.) If you have fewer than 35 years, those no-income years count as zero earnings in this calculation; if you had earnings for more than 35 years, the years of lowest earnings are dropped.

Bottom line: The more taxes you paid into the system, the higher your benefit when you start collecting. As discussed in Section I, the final amount of your benefit is indexed and tied to the prevailing wage rate when you (and all those born in the same year) reach age 60; thereafter your benefit amount is adjusted for inflation (if any) each year in January.

This benefit amount is available when you reach Full Retirement Age (FRA), currently age 66 for those reaching that age in 2017. We can start our benefit anytime between ages 62 and 70. However, for each month that we claim earlier than FRA our benefit is reduced slightly; each month we postpone claiming after FRA up to age 70 increases the benefit amount. While the amounts of the monthly benefit reductions before FRA and increases afterwards vary slightly depending on which month we are talking about, for most practical purposes the month-to-month changes are roughly the same.

For someone whose FRA is 66, making a claim at age 62 reduces the amount by 25%; waiting to age 70 increases the FRA amount by 32%. Here's the most important point to keep in mind: Your age-70 benefit is about 76% greater than your age 62-benefit (plus all the inflation that occurred between ages 62 and 70). That's a big difference: a 76% pay raise in constant dollars for the rest of your life as a reward for waiting to age 70 to claim. As we saw in the last chapter, most people will live long enough for it to be a much better choice to wait to claim.

Example: Margaret was born in 1954. Her FRA is 66. When she reaches FRA her benefit is $2,000. If she starts at age 62 it is reduced 25% to $1,500; if she waits to age 70 it is increased 32% to $2,640, which is 76% more than her age-62 benefit. (Of course, the actual amount at age 70 would be a larger number because all the inflation between 62 and 70 is added to her benefit amount; however, the purchasing power of that age-70 amount will be 76% greater than if she had started her benefit at age 62.)

(For those born in 1955 or later for whom your FRA is between 66 and two months and 67, the reduction from your FRA benefit amount if you claim at 62 is slightly greater; similarly, the increase to age 70 from FRA is slightly less. Most importantly, however, the overall difference between an age-62 claim and an age-70 claim is still about 76% before adjustments for inflation.)

➤ **Spouse Benefits:** When the Social Security program was first created in the 1930s, most married couples consisted of a breadwinner and a homemaker. The original policymakers were concerned that such a couple would have unreasonable difficulty getting by on just one benefit earned by the breadwinner. Thus the spouse benefit (or marital benefit) was born. The homemaker is eligible to receive a partial benefit based on the breadwinner's work record.

It works like this: When the homemaker reaches Full Retirement Age (FRA), he or she is eligible to receive a benefit equal to 50% of what the breadwinner is eligible to receive at his or her FRA. In addition, and under current regulations, the breadwinner must be collecting their work-based benefit in order for the spouse to start a spouse benefit.

As with a work-based benefit, the spouse benefit is also reduced for each month that it is claimed before FRA, up to a maximum of 30% for those claiming at 62 (who have an FRA of 66). However, there is no increase in the amount of the spouse benefit for waiting past FRA, so it should always be claimed by that age if possible.

Example: Jennifer is a homemaker who did not work enough to qualify for Social Security benefits based on her own work record. Her husband Robert is collecting a benefit on his work record in the amount of $1,800 since he reached his FRA of 66. Jennifer's FRA is also 66. If she starts a spouse claim at that age it will be $900 per month, 50% of what Robert was eligible to receive at his FRA. If Jennifer claims as early as age 62 her benefit is reduced to 35% of Robert's FRA benefit, which is $630 per month. The amount increases a bit each month until it reaches the maximum of $900 at FRA. There is no benefit to Jennifer for waiting past FRA to start her spouse benefit because it will not increase past FRA.

➢ **Survivor Benefits:** When the first partner in a married couple passes away the survivor is eligible to receive an amount at least equal to the higher of the two benefits for the remainder of their life. The survivor benefit can be higher than either of the two benefits under one circumstance. If the higher benefit was based on a worker who claimed before FRA, the survivor's benefit amount can be no less than 82.5% of the deceased worker's FRA benefit.

(In other words, if the higher benefit was claimed at age 62 and therefore reduced 25% to be equal to 75% of the FRA benefit, the survivor benefit would be adjusted to be based on 82.5% of the deceased's FRA benefit.)

If the worker has not reached FRA and has not yet filed for their benefit before they pass away, the benefit will equal that worker's FRA benefit; if the deceased is over FRA, the survivor benefit is based on what the deceased would have been eligible to receive as of the month prior to the month that he or she died (up to the maximum of the age 70 benefit).

What if the surviving spouse was not already collecting any benefit? If the survivor is at least age 60, he or she can start a benefit. (The benefit can start as early as age 50 for a survivor who is disabled; benefits can also start earlier for the survivor who has minor children as well as for those minor children. This somewhat-unusual circumstance is beyond the scope of this book.) Note that this age is different from the earliest age (62) to start either work-based or spouse benefits. The reduction factor is different as well: A survivor benefit claimed before FRA is reduced in steady increments to a maximum reduction of 28.5% at age 60. (As if this isn't complicated enough, the FRA table for survivors is slightly different from that for retirees and spouses. If we become a widow or widower a call to the SSA can quickly sort out these details for us. Caution: As we will explain later we will do well to get professional advice regarding claiming our survivor benefits; only call the SSA to learn the amount of the survivor benefit available at various ages.)

OK, that's all a bit tricky. Let's consider an example that illustrates some of these situations.

Example: Don is four years older than Heidi. His work-based FRA benefit is $2,000; hers is $1,600. Don starts his benefit at 62 when it is reduced 25% for early claiming to $1,500. (As we saw in Section I, over 40% start their benefits at 62 and around 90%

claim by the time they reach FRA.) Heidi also starts her benefit at 62, which is reduced 25% from $1,600 to $1,200. Their survivor benefit will be based on the greater of Don's actual benefit ($1,500) or 82.5% of his FRA benefit of $2,000: $1,650. Since $1,650 is greater than $1,500, $1,650 is the amount of the survivor benefit Heidi can receive at or after FRA if Don predeceases her. (If he predeceases her, he would just continue to receive his benefit since it is already greater than any survivor benefit based on her work record.)

Once they both start collecting their benefits they receive a combined $2,700 per month. Don lives to his average life expectancy of about 83. Heidi is 79; she lives another seven years to her average life expectancy of 90. Her survivor benefit is $1,650 per month for all those years (plus any intervening annual inflation adjustments).

Suppose Don passed away when he was 64. Heidi is 60 and she qualifies to collect a survivor benefit. Although Don started his benefit at 62, the survivor benefit amount is based on Don's FRA benefit amount reduced by 28.5% because Heidi is claiming it before her FRA; the benefit amount is $1,430. Heidi is well advised to start this claim at 60. Why? The survivor benefit is already greater than her age-62 work-based benefit of $1,200, yet she can start it two years earlier. She can continue to collect this amount until she turns 70; at that age she can switch to her work-based claim, which has grown 32% from her FRA amount to $2,112. This illustrates a special characteristic of survivor benefits compared to work-based and spouse benefits: if eligible for both (either now or at some later date) we can elect one now and switch to the other one later.

Note that if Heidi is still working at age 60 and up until her FRA, her receipt of benefits is subject to the earnings test limits. Under Social Security's rules we are free to work and collect any benefit for which we are eligible after FRA. Before FRA, however, we are limited in what we can earn and still collect benefits. In 2017 we

WARNING: Survivor Trap

We must be exceedingly careful in exercising a survivor benefit when we have dual eligibility. Suppose Don passes away when Heidi is 62 instead of 60. The survivor benefit would be reduced 19% (instead of 28.5%) to $1,620. Suppose, furthermore, that Heidi's FRA benefit is $2,400. Her reduced work benefit at 62 would be 25% less, or $1,800. It is quite possible for the agent at the Social Security Administration to point out to Heidi that she can collect $180 more by claiming her work claim at that time, locking her into that reduced benefit level for the rest of her life.

If instead Heidi tells the SSA that she wants to restrict her claim to survivor benefits, she will receive $180 less until she is 70, leaving $17,280 on the table during those eight years. However, when she turns 70 she switches to her work benefit, which has grown to $3,168 a month, $1,548 more per month thereafter. That's $18,576 more per year—she recovers what she left on the table in just one year! If she lives to her *average* life expectancy, over 16 more years she collects an additional $278,000. All that extra income would be lost if her claim is improperly entered at age 62. A dual entitlement claim could be financially ruinous. And after one year it would no longer be possible to undo the damage. Sadly, this situation is more common than it should be and deprives many elderly—mostly women—of substantial sums that could make all the difference over the remaining years of their live. (Source: *http://www.pbs.org/newshour/making-sense/social-security-staffer-blows-whistle-systems-treatment-widows/*)

can earn up to $16,920 yearly ($1,410/month)[76] and collect our full benefits; for each $2 we earn above this amount, we lose $1 in benefits up to the point where the entire benefit is clawed back. In the year in which we reach FRA these limits are loosened substantially. Keep in mind that for any months in which any of the benefit is reduced (or taken back), our benefit at FRA is increased as if we had not claimed for that month or months—so over time there is the likelihood that the clawed back benefit is recovered over time because of the benefit increase adjustment.

Going back to the original example in which Don and Heidi live to their average life expectancies, what if Don waits to age 70 to start his benefit? He would collect his maximum potential benefit in the amount of $2,640 per month; this sum would also be the survivor benefit. That's $990 more per month, compared with claiming at 62; $11,880 more per year for Heidi if he predeceases her (compared with his claiming at 62). For the seven additional years that Heidi lives after Don dies, she receives over $83,000 more in benefits if he waits to claim. How much peace of mind does that extra $1,000 per month buy for Heidi as she gets older? What if she needs that money to maintain a decent standard of living? What's she going to do? Go back to work? She's in her 80s!

Moreover, wouldn't Don want that extra money for Heidi after he is gone? While we love to kid about our long-lasting relationships, the truth is most baby boomer couples are genuinely fond of each other. Sure, for a small number of them an extra $1,000 a month won't matter that much, and for a comparably small number they simply cannot afford to wait to claim later. For the vast majority of us? That extra $1,000 in guaranteed income, month after month, year after year, adjusted for inflation, can make all the difference in the world, whether it's about eliminating difficult choices between food, shelter, or medicine, or just in providing an extra measure of peace of mind to know that those awful choices are further at bay.

---

76 https://www.ssa.gov/news/press/factsheets/colafacts2017.pdf

The survivor rules are poorly understood and poorly appreciated, given the enormous impact they can have on the survivor's financial security. And let's get real in this conversation: When we talk about the survivor we are almost always talking about the wife. Yes, there are widowers out there, but there just aren't nearly as many as there are widows. Based on the current claiming behavior of most men, these widows are getting shafted. We need to understand why so that we don't put our wives in an unnecessary predicament.

Unlike earlier generations comprised of breadwinners and home-makers, most baby boomers are dual-earner couples. Still, the fact is that for whatever historical reasons most high earners in those couples are men. That means that when he claims early, she ends up short-changed more often than not. The tragedy is that most men—and women—are ignorant of this impact when they claim their benefits; the problem doesn't appear until years and years later when it's too late to do anything about it.

When I speak publicly on Social Security claiming strategy I often have men come up to me afterward and express gratitude for explaining the negative impact that early claiming could have on their wives. Each one appreciates how she put up with him for all these years and the last thing he would want to do would be to leave her shortchanged.

Wives also come up to express gratitude: They plan to make sure he stays away from the Social Security claims office until he is much closer to 70!

That's how couples react to getting educated on survivor benefits, and that's how it should be.

Bottom line: The spouse who can qualify for the highest age-70 benefit should almost always wait to claim at that age—or literally die trying—because this is the benefit that the survivor will have to live on for the rest of his or her life—usually hers.

By the way: If you otherwise qualify for survivor benefits now or at some time in the future, you will lose those rights if you remarry before age 60. Marry after age 60 and you can keep them and even switch later to your benefits (or a spouse benefit on your new spouse) if that becomes more advantageous.

OK, those are the basic rules that cover about 98% of situations. There are other benefits like family benefits that can apply in unusual circumstances, such as if you reach age 62 and have a minor child or if you have parents without any benefits who depend on you. These are unusual and complex circumstances. Set an appointment with your local office to see how these may apply to your situation.

Next, let's take a look at a number of examples to help develop insights into how these rules play out in practice.

Key Takeaways

There are three basic circumstances that can make us eligible for benefits now or in the future: (1) work record: We worked and paid enough into the Social Security system in taxes to qualify when we get old enough; (2) spouse: We are at least 62 and married at least a year to someone eligible under their work record who has started to collect their benefits (or divorced after a minimum 10 years of marriage, whether or not the former spouse started their benefit after age 62); and (3) survivor: We are at least 60 (50 if we are disabled) and were married at least nine months (there are exceptions that shorten this) to someone eligible under their Work Record, whether they started their benefits or not (or divorced after a minimum 10 years of marriage, and not remarried before age 60).

These various routes to eligibility can interact in complex ways. To get the most out of our benefits we need to understand how they interact. When in doubt talk to an independent consultant who specializes in Social Security; don't rely solely on information or advice from the Social Security Administration, which, however well intentioned, can be misleading or wrong—and hence costly if we depend on it alone.

No Alarm Clock Needed
in Cotacachi, Ecuador
By Wendy DeChambeau, *InternationalLiving.com*

When asked what they like most about their new life in the small mountain town of Cotacachi, Ecuador, Jay and Nancy Kettering reply, "No alarm clock!" The couple escaped their busy corporate jobs in 2014 and can be found still enjoying everything that life in the high Andes offers…a slow pace of life, fresh produce, low-cost healthcare, and great living for under $2,000 a month.

In their past lives in Denver, Jay worked in the service department of a Nissan dealership, and Nancy was an account manager at a business psychology company. But the couple is happy to report that their lives are now far less hectic.

"We often wake up whenever we feel like it; brew a pot of coffee; enjoy the nice morning; get breakfast; do some reading; check the news on the internet; and maybe watch some videos," says Jay.

"Other times we meet friends for lunch, go to local festivals and parades, or go exploring other towns with friends," says Nancy.

Some of their new daily routine, like morning visits to the local gym, was interrupted when Nancy broke her ankle this past summer. While dealing with health problems is never fun, Nancy has nothing but good things to say about the medical care she received at a private clinic in the nearby city of Ibarra. "The whole experience was smooth, everyone was professional, it was better than any experience we had in the States. We figured absolutely everything from start to finish, including taxi fees, doctor fees, X-rays, the casts, and the walking boot, all came to $400."

Healthcare was one of the main reasons why the couple chose Ecuador. "Even though we're in good health, finding a country with good-quality healthcare was important to us and included in our list of things we were looking for," says Nancy.

Like many prospective expats, they faced a difficult choice in narrowing down which country would be their new home. Nicaragua, Panama, Mexico, and Belize were all contenders. But in the end, the highlands of Ecuador won out.

Nancy's research showed that a budget of $2,000 a month would be enough to live well in Cotacachi. Now that they're here, she estimates that they spend even less. They pay $550 for a partially furnished, two-bedroom townhouse just outside town, up to $30 for electricity, and $5 or $6 for gas each month. Their largest regular expense is internet, for which they pay $110 a month but feel is worth it for fast and dependable service.

They also feel the cost of dining out can't be beat here. "I think eating out is sometimes almost cheaper than buying groceries and cooking at home. We like going to the *Mercado* (market) for lunch, and that costs maybe $2.50 or $3 apiece," says Nancy.

In most respects they couldn't have asked for an easier transition abroad. However, there was one major bump during the moving process, which the couple feels other prospective expats could learn from. "I was naïve and thought Maggie [their black lab] could just fly as cargo on the plane with us. But the airline was horrendous in helping, and I wish I had researched other airlines that were more pet-friendly in advance."

Luckily, everything else went off without a hitch. "Our move here was very easy and getting our visas was very easy," Nancy says. "We used a lawyer and paid $2,200 for both of us (which included the visa and lawyer's fees), and our visas were ready before we ever left the States. The whole process was so smooth."

CHAPTER 10
The Devil in the Dual Entitlement Details

My goal in writing this book is to help you understand how Social Security works so that you can create the best claiming strategy in order to get all you deserve in retirement. The lifestyle you want is within your grasp, but you need to be proactive to get your benefits to your full advantage. That's why I've been trying to educate you about the ins-and-outs of Social Security, including using some terms that might get confusing.

There are two terms in particular that often seem interchangeable, though in the context of Social Security each has a distinct meaning: "eligible" and "entitled." We are eligible for a benefit once we qualify for all the rules; we are entitled once we have made a proper filing to start collecting that benefit. We continue to be so entitled as long as we continue receiving the benefit. This is an important distinction for the following reason: We do not want to make a filing that applies for more than one benefit—dual entitlement—when our intention is to file for only one of the benefits to which we are eligible at that time. Why? Because once we file for both benefits we can no longer switch to the other benefit later. We saw an example of this potential problem in the prior chapter (under "Survivor Trap").

Any spouse who is qualified to receive a work-based benefit is or will be subject to dual eligibility. In addition to the work-based benefit they will also be eligible at some point to receive a spouse benefit. Under current rules, when we apply for our benefits sometime at or after age 62 the Social Security Administration (SSA) will look to see if we have dual eligibility. If we do, the SSA will calculate the potential amount of each benefit (as adjusted for any reductions for claiming before FRA or deferred credits for claiming after FRA) and grant us an amount equal to the greater of the two benefits. (This is an important distinction in contrast with survivor benefits, by which we can elect to take the survivor benefit now if we are eligible, then we can switch at a later date to a work-based benefit that can grow in value in the meantime. That election is not available for spouse and work-based benefits, except for those grandfathered in pursuant to the Bipartisan Budget Act of November 2015 as discussed later in this chapter.)

Carla and Sean: A Case of Dual Eligibility

Recall, however, that to become entitled to a spouse benefit your spouse must have already filed with the Social Security Administration and be collecting a work-based benefit. (There are some notable, if increasingly rare, exceptions to this rule that we will cover later.)

Example: Carla and Sean are both 66, their Full Retirement Age. She qualifies for an FRA benefit of $800, based on her work record. He qualifies for an FRA benefit of $2,000, based on his work record. He is (wisely, in our view) waiting until later to start his work-based claim, which will grow 32% to $2,640 at age 70, thereby locking in the couple's highest-possible survivor benefit.

Carla decides to start her benefit now. Because Sean has not yet started collecting a claim, he is not registered in the system in a way that allows a spouse claim, so Carla's benefit is based solely on her work-based claim, and she is entitled to receive $800. When Sean turns 70 and starts collecting his benefit, Carla becomes dually entitled and the SSA will award her a benefit increase of $200, to $1,000 per month. Why? Her spouse claim is based on 50% of what Sean was eligible to receive at his FRA, whether he starts at that age or not, and Carla is now eligible to receive an amount equal to the higher of the two benefits because Sean is now entered in the system.

The sharp reader will note that if Sean chose instead to start his benefit at age 66, Carla would have been dually eligible and been entitled to receive $1,000 a month at that time. As a result of Sean waiting to age 70 to start his benefit, she collects $200 a month less for 48 months, a total of $9,600 left on the table. This is an added cost of the trade-off for Sean waiting to claim at age 70. While each couple needs to weigh these trade-offs based on their own situation, we take the view that locking in the higher survival benefit is worth waiting for. It will be easier (not to say it will be easy) for them to get by on $200 less in their late 60s than for the survivor to get by on $640 less per month for however long they live.

Here's the kicker, though: The benefit increase due to Carla when Sean starts collecting is not automatic! Under certain circumstances the SSA will fail to recognize the dual eligibility and will not grant it unless Carla or Sean brings it to their attention. (We started the book off with a real case like this.) Suppose Carla realizes when she turns 71 that she should have been receiving $1,000. The SSA will grant a retroactive adjustment of six months of lost benefits, and Carla and Sean will be out of luck on the first six months. Not all benefits are automatic. For some you have to proactively prod the SSA to get it right.

What if Sean is four years older than Carla and starts his work-based benefit at age 70? Then Carla enjoys dual entitlement at age 66 when she applies and would receive the $1,000-per-month spouse benefit amount at that time.

Why You Should let the SSA Handle the Calculations

Let's consider what happens if instead Carla starts her benefit at 62 while Sean, four years older, waits to age 70. Since dual eligibility does not yet apply, her work-based benefit is reduced by 25% from the FRA amount. Twenty-five percent of $800 is a $200 reduction, so the award amount would be $600. What happens four years later when Sean starts his age-70 benefit? Carla becomes dually eligible to both work- and spouse-based benefits. Because she has now reached FRA, Carla applies and is entitled to receive an increase equal to the difference between her FRA spouse benefit of $1,000 and her own FRA benefit of $800: $1,000 - $800 = $200. Add this to the $600 she is receiving for a new total of $800.

The case of Carla and Sean brings up an important consideration particular to any couple's circumstances: the age difference, if any. Suppose, for instance, that Carla is four years older than Sean. If she starts her reduced work-based benefit at 62 in the amount of $600, she would have to wait 12 years to age 74 to shift to her spouse claim when Sean turns 70 and files his claim.

Did you follow all that? We didn't either. And we wrote it...

The good news is that it is not important to understand that calculation or the rules determining Carla's amount(s). What is important is to understand that dual eligibility may apply to you at some point. Moreover, in Carla's situation it is not automatic that she will get the increase when Sean starts his benefit. The SSA may ask whether he has a spouse when Sean makes his application; it should, that's its policy. However, that does not guarantee that it will happen, and I can tell you that I have worked with couples in whose situations such an increase did not happen when the second spouse went to file—the couple had to go to the SSA after the fact to get the benefit increase for which they were eligible.

For most of us that was a somewhat mind-numbing calculation and not one that we want to have to deal with. However, it is a useful example in helping us to understand that it's a fool's game to try to understand all the intricacies of the SSA's regulations. What we need to know is how to manage our interactions with the SSA in such a way that we learn what our options are and when they apply. Let the SSA deal with the calculations; it is actually very good at this part of its job. In Chapter 11 we provide a summary guide for identifying and managing your benefit rights.

Unusual Claiming Issues

Before we proceed to the summary guide, we need to cover several special regulations that apply to many, though not most, people. First we'll identify who needs to be concerned.

These may apply if you or your spouse:

1. Worked much or most of your career for a public entity (usually city, county, or state government or as teachers) and they did not withhold Social Security taxes from your paycheck. Some states have this kind of pension; others have pensions even though they also paid Social Security taxes on that income (in which case they can collect both their pension and Social Security benefits). You know if you didn't pay any of these taxes for most of your career, even if you might have had some other jobs in which you did pay Social Security taxes.

2. You are married, are eligible for a work-based claim that you plan to wait to start after age 66, have a spouse eligible for a work-based claim, and you turned 66 in time to "file and suspend" collection of your benefit with the Social Security Administration before April 29, 2016.

3. You are married (or were for at least 10 years and have not remarried) to someone eligible for a work-based claim, you are eligible for your own work-based claim, and you were born on or before January 1, 1954.

None of these apply to you? Move on to Chapter 11. This information is of no relevance to you. The rest of you, read on…

WEP and GPO

If you worked for a public entity (item No. 1 above) where you did not pay any Social Security taxes, you are subject to two regulations: the Windfall Elimination Provision (WEP) and the Government Pension

Offset (GPO). These apply when, in addition to your government job(s), you had other jobs during your career that also make you eligible to collect a Social Security benefit. The WEP rule reduces your Social Security benefit by half of your non-Social Security pension up to a maximum of $428 (2016 rate). Depending on how many years you paid Social Security taxes, the deduction phases out between 20 and 30 years paying into the system.

The GPO rule reduces any spouse or survivor benefit you might otherwise be eligible for from your spouse. To the extent that your spouse or survivor benefit exceeds two-thirds of your pension, you can collect the excess; if it does not exceed two-thirds of your pension you cannot collect anything.

This brief discussion is more to make you aware of this issue than to provide comprehensive coverage of these rules. More information is available at this link: *https://www.ssa.gov/planners/retire/gpo-wep.html*.

Laidback, Affordable Beach-Living in Beautiful Belize
By Ann Kuffner, *InternationalLiving.com*

In November 2011, Patrick Snyder made his first trip to Belize, to visit his brother. Planning to spend a month, he stayed for seven. He then returned home, took care of his personal affairs, packed his belongings, and returned to Belize in 2012.

"I like the peace and quiet in Punta Gorda, and the slow pace of life. I enjoy being right on the bay. People here are friendly. I live simply and it's been easy to make new friends. At this point in my life, I could not ask for more."

Patrick had been living in the lower mainland region of British Columbia. He and his wife owned and operated a chain of women's clothing stores. Before that he'd worked as an engineer for Hydro Quebec, as well as for oil and natural gas companies.

But Patrick's life took a turn when his wife passed away in 2011. Still healthy himself, Patrick pondered how to spend the rest of his life… Then his brother, Lea, convinced Patrick to visit him in Belize for a change of scenery. "My brother told me to 'get a life'. I visited him in Hopkins in October of 2011, planning to spend a month. I ended up staying much longer." After returning to Canada for a few months, Patrick decided to return to Belize.

Once there, Lea asked him for a favor. He wondered if Patrick would be willing to check out Punta Gorda for him, to determine if it would be worthwhile opening an office there for his business. Patrick was so smitten by the region that he decided to remain there. Before long, Patrick was comfortably settled in Punta Gorda, enjoying the tranquil lifestyle in this comfortable, seaside town.

He enjoys the region's mix of cultures—which include Maya, Kriol, East Indian, and Garifuna—and has been quick to learn about their traditions. Since he eats out often, he's met many people at the local restaurants he frequents. Over time, they've become friends.

Patrick finds it easy to meet people while out, "I eat out regularly and meet people in the restaurants I frequent. We have become friends over time. I've found it easy to make friends here."

Because the cost of living is lower in Belize, he enjoys a much better lifestyle than he could afford in Canada. Rent, food, and property are all less expensive in Belize. He budgets $1,500 a month but often spends less. His rent for a one-bedroom house, with a bay view, is only $350 a month. A fresh fish lunch runs him $4. On average he spends only $15 a day eating all three meals at local restaurants.

And there's no need for a car, either. "I walk a lot. I also ride my bike around town. And I have a scooter. I feel very safe walking around town, even late at night. I walk regularly to Walucos or other local restaurants to meet friends for dinner and a drink."

Punta Gorda—and southern Belize in general—was once a cradle of Maya civilization, and Patrick has visited several of the spectacular ruins nearby. He also gets out into the bay once in a while for a pleasant boat ride, or some fishing. But he's not interested in demanding athletic activities. He's settled into a comfortable lifestyle that's peaceful, contemplative, and social…

At heart, Patrick's a creative guy. As a young man he yearned to become a writer/artist. And now he has the time to indulge his favorite creative pursuits, especially writing poetry. (He's working on a series of poems and has written a few about his adopted home country.)

Patrick says it's easy and inexpensive to keep in touch with his son back home and with other relatives online, via MagicJack.

He returns to Canada for a few months every year, and some family members are also planning trips to visit him in Belize. And his brother Lea still lives in nearby Hopkins.

Patrick has no regrets about his decision to move to Belize. "I have many good memories of home. But this is a new life. I've turned the page." He has enjoyed his time in Belize. But he also now has the confidence to consider options for a new adventure…

The Bipartisan Budget Act of 2015

This legislation, passed in November 2015, eliminated certain Social Security claiming options for everyone except those who fall within the criteria of Nos. 2 and 3 above.

If you fit within these criteria this could be very important to you: possibly tens of thousands of extra dollars that you or your spouse

may be able to collect. This benefit is so sweet that Congress eliminated it for everyone else who is younger because it believes it was too generous. So don't miss out on this.

OK, hopefully I have your attention.

If you are the spouse who fits the criteria of No. 2, then it means you reached age 66 (Full Retirement Age) in time to "file and suspend" collection of your benefits with SSA by the filing deadline of April 29, 2016, as established under the Bipartisan Budget Act.

Why file and suspend? In doing so you became registered into the SSA system as an active beneficiary (entitled), yet by immediately suspending receipt of any benefits you are able receive the deferred retirement credits (DRCs) that permit your work-based benefit value to continue to grow 8% per year up to age 70; in addition, by being registered in the system as a beneficiary, you also open the door for your spouse to make a very special claim…

Supplemental Spouse Claim

If you were born on or before Jan. 1, 1954 (No. 3 above), and your spouse was able to file and suspend at age 66 (pursuant to No. 2 above), or your spouse has already started a work-based benefit, you have a unique option when you reach your FRA, which is 66. You will become eligible at that time to file a "restricted" (that's a key word to use when applying) application in which you receive a spouse benefit based on your spouse's work record. The amount equals 50% of what your spouse is eligible to receive at their FRA (whether they start to collect at that time, earlier or later).

This is especially valuable for working couples whose benefit amounts are in the same ballpark. Why? Because you can collect this benefit for 48 months while you are waiting for your own work-based benefit to grow 32% more than it would be if you claimed it at 66. (To the extent your work-based benefit is much lower than your spouse's work-based benefit, this strategy may not yield much extra benefit, if any. You want to examine the numbers carefully to be certain.)

Suppose your FRA benefit is $1,600 and your spouse's is $2,000. At your FRA you file a restricted claim and receive 50% of your spouse's FRA benefit of $2,000. That's $1,000 a month you collect for 48 months, or $48,000. While you collect this benefit your own work-based benefit grows 32%, from $1,600 to $2,112, and you switch to that amount when you turn 70. In other words, you are essentially rewarded an extra $48,000 in benefits for waiting to allow your own work-based claim to reach its maximum value at age 70.

Sweet, right? You bet it is—so sweet that Congress has cancelled it for everyone born after Jan. 1, 1954. Don't miss out on this if you are among those grandfathered in who qualify. When in doubt get professional advice.

CAUTION: One of the reasons Congress was able to get away with removing this benefit without much fuss is that it was not widely known by the public. Because it was not widely known, it was not widely claimed. As a result, staff at SSA are often ignorant of this option. Worse, with the law change, they have received some vague memos to the effect that the option was eliminated. What this means for you—if you qualify—is you may encounter resistance when you go to apply.

Recently I have had clients with a range of experiences. Some had an agent who knew exactly what they were talking about, verified their eligibility and signed them right up. Others have been repeatedly told that they could not do this, that they did not qualify (when they did) and that the option was no longer available (when it is for some). Recently one client was told "No" three times by three different agents before getting to one who said "Yes." You may need to be persistent in getting to "Yes" in order to cash in on this valuable benefit while it still lasts.

Key Takeaways

In the prior chapter we saw that there are several circumstances that can make us eligible for Social Security benefits: work record, spouse, and survivor. In this chapter we waded into the complexity that arises when we become eligible for more than one benefit, either now or in the future. While at times we can use this dual eligibility to our financial advantage, we also want to make sure we exercise these options in a manner that serves us best.

We also looked at some unusual claiming circumstances. If you did not see yourself reflected in those particular circumstances, ignore them. If you did, make careful note to understand—or get further educated about—how the rules apply to you before you file any claims.

CHAPTER 11
Just the Facts, Ma'am, Just the Facts...

The purpose of this chapter is to provide a brief guide for how and when to obtain the information we need to develop and manage our Social Security claiming strategy. If we follow these steps we should be able to reduce the chance of making a claiming error or of losing out on benefits to which we might otherwise be entitled at some point in time. We've already looked at a number of instances like this so far in this book and we want to avoid those mistakes for ourselves. They can cost us the kind of retirement we're hoping for.

Know Our Benefit Amounts

As we saw earlier in Chapter 7, for nearly all of us, our Social Security benefits are our most valuable asset—more valuable than our savings and retirement accounts and more valuable than the equity in our home. Just as we have to manage our other financial assets, we also need to manage our benefits. This starts by knowing what they are.

As long as we have our 40 quarters (10 years) of paying Social Security taxes, we qualify for benefits. The Social Security Administration used to send out annual statements once we reached this threshold that provided benefit estimates as well as details of all the income we earned that was subject to Social Security taxes. Now it sends those only every decade (at 30, 40, and 50) and annually after age 59 until we claim. It's easy to miss this in the mail.

Today, however, it is easy and reliable to simply go online anytime to find out the current estimate of our benefits. Here's how to do that:

How to Get Your Estimate from the Social Security Administration Website

The Social Security Administration (SSA) provides several ways to find your estimated Social Security benefit at Full Retirement Age (FRA). One is the paper statement mentioned above. Another is to visit the SSA website to use its online estimator. You provide some information that will identify you. The site will access your Social Security earnings record and tell you what it estimates you will receive when you start collecting Social Security retirement benefits.

Here's how to do this. I suggest you do it right now as your read through the steps:

1. Go to the official SSA Estimator link here: *www.ssa.gov/estimator/*.

2. Scroll down to and click on the "Estimate Your Retirement Benefits" button.

3. On the next page enter your name, other last name (if the one on your most recent Social Security card is different than the last name you first entered), your maiden name (if applicable), mother's maiden name, Social Security Number, date of birth, and place of birth (select from a drop-down list).

4. On the same page, review the "Terms of Service." If these terms are acceptable to you, check the box that says "I agree to the Terms of Service" and click on the button that says "Submit."

(Be aware that at this point you might encounter a discrepancy between what you think is your identifying information and what the SSA has in its files. After three "tries" you will be frozen out of the account if there is still a problem. It happens. It happened to me. You will have to visit a local office where you will be required to provide sufficient documentation to establish your identity to the SSA's satisfaction. It can require more than one visit. While this will be annoying if it happens to you, keep in mind that this is part of the administration's effort to protect you and keep anyone else from ever being able to hack your account. If there is such a problem, better to find out about it and sort it out sooner rather than later.)

5. In the next screen enter your earnings from last year in the box below "Last year's earnings." The SSA asks you to provide this information because of the delay in the IRS providing this information to the SSA. Providing this number results in a more accurate estimate of your future benefits. However, don't waste time looking for the exact number in your tax returns. Just put in your best guess. Even if you are off by a large amount, it won't make much difference in the estimate. Now click the button that says "Next."

The next screen will provide the current estimate of your Full Retirement Age benefit, along with the amount of earnings that this estimate assumes you will earn each year until that age. The next row provides the current estimate of your age-70 benefit with the same earnings assumption. The last row provides your age 62-benefit with the same assumption on earnings (unless you are already older than 62, in which case it returns your benefit amount if you file now).

You can print the page for future easy reference. Note that there is no personal information such as your name or Social Security Number on the page—just the benefit amounts at various ages and the related earnings assumptions. The whole process takes no more than a few minutes. Repeat for your spouse.

Here's another valuable exercise to do while logged into the SSA Estimator: You can run another scenario by clicking the "Add a New Estimate." Most people do not plan to work until they are 70, and they rightly wonder how much it will affect their benefits if they stop having any earnings before they start collecting. You can enter the age at which you plan to stop working, and you can then enter the amount of earnings you expect to have up to that age. Click the "Submit" button and the SSA will re-compute your future benefit estimates accordingly. You can pursue this exercise as many times as you like. Usually we are surprised to learn how little working more or fewer years changes the benefit estimate. Once we have put 30-plus years into the work force our benefit doesn't vary much with additional earnings.

This exercise is especially helpful when creating budgets for our retirement plans and when we want to run "What if?" scenarios for when we might stop working and when we might start collecting. We will revisit this topic again in the next section on planning an overseas retirement.

Monitor Your Earnings History

Another way to get a current estimate of your benefits is to create a "my Social Security" account on the SSA website. In addition to benefit estimates you can also review your earnings history (as it has been reported to the SSA by the IRS) on a regular basis.

Why is this important? We want to be sure that all of our earnings have been reported to the SSA. Some unscrupulous employers may deduct our taxes from our paycheck but fail to report this to the IRS (they pocket the money). While that is harder to do in this day and age, I can tell you it happened to me early in my working career, long before you could go online to check on this. I lost out on the taxes withheld from my checks in that year. You have to raise questions in a timely manner in order to get your record corrected. It takes just a few minutes every year or two to go online and check this if you are early in your career. Do it.

Setting up an account is also valuable for managing your benefits once you start collecting. You can designate the financial institution where your benefit is paid, get related tax forms, and request a letter as proof of the benefits you receive. This latter service is essential for most people when applying for various types of residence visas for many countries where proof of a minimum amount of monthly income is required. Social Security benefits are recognized nearly everywhere for this purpose.

You can get a more comprehensive list of services available through a "my Social Security" account and sign up at this link: *www.ssa.gov/myaccount/*.

Give Them a Call

You can speak with an agent at the Social Security Administration by phone by calling *1-800-772-1213*. This is a 24-hour automated system where they try to answer your questions without actually having you speak to anyone. Often that may be enough. However, if you want to speak to someone the lines are staffed between 7:00 a.m. and 8:00 p.m. for your local time, Monday through Friday excluding holidays. To escape the phone tree ask an impossible question that the computer voice cannot process: "Why is the sky blue at Social Security?" You will soon be told to "Please hold while we find someone who can help you." There is usually a wait time and they will tell you how long it is; then they will offer to call you back within a certain amount of time. That option works very well in my experience. You just need to stay near your phone to take the return call.

Once you reach an agent they will verify your identity, much as they do online. Then they can provide you basically the same information you can see online. The problem arises if you get into a further conversation with them. The reliability of their answers varies all over the place, again in my experience and that of my clients. Be cautious with whatever you are told. Agents are encouraged to make us aware of any benefits for which we might be eligible right then and there and then offer to sign us up. That may or may not be in our best interests (usually not). From their point of view they would rather get us into the system at that time so we don't take up any more of their time in the future. Staffing the phones costs money and Congress puts pressure on the agency to constantly look for ways to cut those costs.

Summary Guide for Determining
Your Claiming Options

Single, married, divorced, remarried, widow, widower… As we see by now there are simply too many possible claiming combinations to cover everyone's situation in one book. We don't even try. Instead, our goal is to provide access to the right information and the right questions to ask at the right time. Now we try to distill this into a summary guide for future reference.

Rules of Thumb: Most were covered before, though a few are new to this list. Here they are all in one abbreviated space. Some may apply to us now and others later as our life circumstances change. We need to remember to revisit this list when those changes occur, update our numbers by visiting our records at the Social Security website, and revise our claiming plans accordingly.

➤ If you haven't already, look up the amount of your work-based benefit at your FRA. This is a fundamental piece of information for any financial planning you will do, so it is worth knowing at least by your mid-to-late 50s.

➤ If married understand whether and under what circumstances a spouse entitlement may become available to either of you. You have to be married at least one year to qualify for a spouse benefit (nine months for a survivor's benefit—though there are exceptions that can shorten this time).

➤ You can initiate your benefit claim 90 days prior to the month in which you want those benefits to start. It's wise to start early so there is plenty of time to address and correct any issues that may come up during the process. For now (writing in early 2017) I recommend making an appointment and applying in person at a branch office. (I encounter too many problems involving applications submitted online or by phone.) Once you submit a claim that is accepted you will receive written confirmation of the amount you will be paid and when payment starts (an "award letter"). (If the claim is rejected—unlikely if you applied in person or by phone since they would point out any problem at that time—you will be sent a "denial letter" with an explanation of what is needed to complete the application.) **Be sure that any award letter accurately reflects your understanding of the benefits you expect to receive. Otherwise you can misunderstand and be locked into a claiming strategy for the rest of your life that is suboptimal. When in doubt get professional advice to help you review the SSA letter.**

➢ If single, beginning at age 62, anytime you can look in the mirror and think, "Yeah, I could live another dozen years or so," delay starting a work-based claim for at least a year. Repeat each year up to age 70. There is no increase in benefits for waiting beyond age 70 to claim.

➢ If married and a spouse claim is greater than a work-based claim, don't wait past FRA to start that spouse claim, because it doesn't increase anymore past FRA.

➢ If married, whoever has the highest potential Social Security benefit waits to 70 (or dies trying…) to maximize the survivor's benefit, regardless of the age difference. Exception: If you both have approximately the same benefit level, the older one should wait to age 70 to lock in the highest survivor benefit. For the younger one, look to this rule: If your spouse might live another dozen years or so, wait another year before filing your claim. Repeat each year.

➢ If married and there is a large age difference and the older spouse sets the survivor benefit, it may be best to start a claim at 62. (Note how unusual this is: This is probably the only time we have suggested a reason, besides financial destitution, for claiming early.) Suppose he is 82 and she is 62. She should probably start a spouse- or work-based benefit (whichever she is eligible for) even though it's reduced for early claiming. Why? If she waits till 70 (he is 90) she has collected nothing so far and he is likely to die soon (if he hasn't already passed on). She will immediately begin collecting the higher survivor benefit. As a couple they will probably be better off if she collects at 62.

➤ Marriage Plus: You or your spouse can qualify for a spouse benefit after at least one year of marriage.

➤ Marriage Minus: If you qualify for a spouse claim on an ex-spouse (because you were married at least 10 years), you forfeit that claim if you remarry. However, you may qualify on your new spouse's record after one year. (Exception: If you and your boyfriend/ girlfriend are both collecting a spouse benefit from an ex-spouse, then you can keep that benefit if you get married under certain circumstances.)

➤ Marriage Mixed: If you qualify for a survivor claim on an ex-spouse (because you were married at least 10 years), you forfeit that claim if you remarry before age 60. Marry after and you can keep the claim...and still switch to your new spouse's survivor benefit at their death if it's higher.

➤ Divorce: If a spouse claim based on your spouse's work record could exceed one based on your own work record, consider waiting for the minimum 10 years before finalizing the paperwork, especially if that's only a year or two away. You can be happily separated knowing that you can count on a valuable benefit beginning in your 60s for the rest of your life that won't cost your ex or your ex's new spouse a penny.

➤ Death of a spouse (or ex-spouse to whom you were married at least 10 years): Plan your claiming strategy very carefully. In particular, don't be forced to claim both a survivor claim and a work-based claim simultaneously. Often you can start to collect the survivor benefit at 60 (or current age if older) and switch to your work-based claim at 70. That's impossible if your claim is entered for both benefits at the initial filing age.

➤ If there is any possible question concerning your claim status or options following an interaction with the SSA, thoroughly document your recollection and understanding of the interaction in writing and request a letter of confirmation or clarification. By writing you open a claim window with a date stamp that creates rights to make corrections in a timely manner. If the SSA response raises any questions, get advice on how to proceed before your window of time expires.

➤ The Do-Over: Mistakes happen. Following any initial filing to claim benefits from the SSA we have one year to change our minds and withdraw the application. File Form SSA-521. We also need to repay any benefits we received since our claim. The SSA will calculate this amount for us so we know exactly how much to pay back. Once this is done it is as if we never filed in the first place. We can do this only once.

➤ Fix a Broken Claiming Strategy: If you learn that you claimed too early and the year has passed to withdraw your claim, you still have an option. At or after FRA you can suspend collection of your benefits, and they will grow in value by 8% per year plus inflation up to age 70, when they will restart. If your FRA is 66, suspending until 70 adds a 32% increase when you reach that age, a hefty raise for the rest of your life that is well worth it if you are in close-to-mediocre-or-better health at that age.

➤ When in doubt, get professional advice: Because benefits can be paid out monthly over decades of our lives, substantial sums of money can be at stake. Claiming errors, therefore, can be costly. Moreover, the SSA agents often tell us that we cannot make the claim we are trying to make when in fact we can. The agent simply isn't familiar with that particular rule. In my experience, the agents are well trained and well intentioned. The problem is with the maze of regulations that can become so complex and obscure; agents rarely encounter these unusual situations and instead spend nearly all their time dealing with simple, standard cases, like determining what your work-based benefit will be at various ages or taking basic application information. When the agent encounters an issue they have not seen before they are stumped. That doesn't mean they won't give you an answer. It just has a greater likelihood of being wrong. A professional can help you direct the agent to the specific regulation that applies to your situation.

Key Takeaways

We covered how to get the current estimate of our benefits either online at *www.ssa.gov/estimator/* or by phone: *1-800-772-1213*. We can also review our earnings history as reported to the Social Security Administration by setting up an account at *www.ssa.gov/myaccount/*.

Then we provided a **Summary Guide for Determining Your Claiming Options**. Since we can't effectively summarize a summary, it's a good idea to just bookmark this section for future quick reference.

Enjoying a Carefree Life on a Social Security Budget

By Ed O'Connor, *InternationalLiving.com*

My journey to Cuenca, Ecuador began with a discussion with friends in their home by the beach in Panama. We were all disenchanted with the U.S.—the regulations, the taxes… We concluded that there's no American dream anymore.

My wife, Olga, who was raised in the Soviet Union told me that she felt she had more freedom there than in the U.S. Quite an eye-opening statement for me to hear.

Not long after our return to Pennsylvania where I was employed as a driver recruiter for a transportation company my employer told me he no longer needed my services. Then the day after Labor Day we lost our home and all of our possessions in a flood.

While staying in the home of some friends for a month after the flood, I came across a copy of *International Living* magazine with an article about Cuenca, Ecuador. I knew Ecuador was in South America and the capital was Quito but that was the extent of my knowledge. So I did some internet research and read books about Ecuador and retiring abroad.

In the meantime I'd applied for dozens of jobs without getting one interview. Olga and I decided it was time for a change. We left Pennsylvania for Cuenca with nine pieces of luggage and a lot of hope.

Today, we live in this beautiful, affordable city, surrounded by its many majestic churches and old buildings, and enjoy a wonderful climate. We are kept entertained by the free performances put on by the Cuenca Symphony, the many museums and theaters, and we're just a 10-minute walk from Inca ruins.

Our only income is my Social Security, but we're living better than we ever have before. We pay $350 a month in rent for our new, 1,616-square-foot, three-bedroom, two-bathroom apartment. And the monthly cost for utilities is equally low: Electricity and trash removal, $12.70…water, $6.61…propane for hot water, gas dryer, and gas stove, $4.64…phone/internet, $30.11.

We don't have a car because we can walk to almost anywhere we need to go. If we use transportation we take the bus or a taxi. Our average monthly transportation costs are around $17.

Food is extremely affordable and we go to the local markets for most of our groceries. We can dine at one of the local eateries for $2 to $4.

Healthcare is also much more affordable. Although we have opted for government insurance in case of emergencies, which costs $84 a month for the two of us with no deductibles or copays, we tend to pay for our doctor and dentist visits out of pocket. They both charge $15 for a visit.

Everyday life here is busy, but in a fun way. Olga goes to a fitness class three times a week, we have Spanish classes twice a week, and we volunteer at Cuenca University to help students with English. Having been in the Air Force, I belong to a veteran's group, I sing with the Cuenca International Chorus and also in our church choir.

Cuenca reminds me of growing up in 1950s and 60s America…there's that freedom to enjoy life the way we want to. We definitely made the right choice in retiring to Cuenca.

SECTION
III

MANAGING CLAIMING STRATEGY FOR A SECURE RETIREMENT

W e've been studying the many pieces that need to be considered to (1) determine those Social Security benefits for which we may become eligible and (2) evaluate how these benefit amounts vary depending on when we start to collect them.

Still, it's just a pile of pieces at this point. This section is designed to begin to put the pieces together to illustrate our larger purpose: To present a variety of cases that demonstrate ways to use claiming strategy to best help bring financial security to our retirement plans. In particular, we want to consider these strategies in the context of an *International Living* lifestyle. (One of the many advantages of Social Security income is that it can go wherever we go. We can arrange to have our payment deposited directly into a variety of correspondent banks in nearly every country around the world—certainly any country that anyone would want to live in. Or we can have our monthly benefit deposited to our U.S. bank and manage the funds from there, much as we do with our other money.)

More specifically the purpose of this section is to quantify how much better off we are likely to be financially as we age if we wait to claim our Social Security benefits later rather than sooner. We will do that by reviewing a variety of stories—we'll call them "cases"—in which we compare the outcomes of different claiming strategies over time. We start each case with a given amount of savings and spending and then look at what happens to the savings as we get older, depending on when we start our Social Security benefits. Spoiler alert! It usually pays to wait…

In the cases that follow, these are the primary "pieces" we will consider:

1. **Social Security:** In general—though not always—we will examine a case in which the beneficiary (or beneficiaries, if married) claim at 62 or wait to claim at age 70. The other pieces (listed below) will have the same starting values for a given case. In other words, for each case we start with the same savings and identical spending plans and so on.

2. **Retirement Savings:** This is money held in accounts such as 401(k)s, IRAs, and the like. When we withdraw this money we will have to pay income tax on it if our adjustable gross income is greater than our standard deductions and exemptions.

3. **Regular Savings:** This is all our other money. Any money we receive from work, pensions, retirement savings withdrawals, net proceeds from the sale of a home, and/or Social Security benefits goes into this account. Living expenses, travel, taxes, property purchases, and any other spending come out of this account. It may also include investment accounts; however, it excludes any retirement (tax-deferred) savings, except when we withdraw from such accounts, either by choice or as part of the Required Minimum Distributions we must take beginning at age 70.

4. **Spending Plan:** This is the all-in spending: relocation costs (counted separately in the first year), housing (our budgets assume renting; if we have the funds to purchase that is because we have more

options—we are focused on limited options), utilities, food, medical (including health insurance), entertainment, travel, income taxes (if any), plus any emergencies.

There are many other pieces we could add to this puzzle: income from a pension or from a job, purchase of a home versus renting, starting a business, and so on. These are all very real possibilities for an *International Living* lifestyle. Indeed, in order to move overseas when we are much younger, another source of income for a number of years until we can start our Social Security benefits might be a necessity. For the purposes of this book, however, we want to keep it simple. We will find that it wouldn't be difficult to imagine modifying any or all of our cases to include one or more of these pieces.

Other Standard Assumptions:

➤ **This is important to note:** All savings (regular or tax-deferred) earn enough to keep up with inflation after any associated taxes on earnings. In other words, while we don't lose money on our investments, we don't earn any in real terms. This is probably overly conservative (although we certainly can lose money on our investments, especially over the near term). However, our concern is not with the upside potential of a financial plan. Instead, our focus is on the downside, to present a plan that is reasonably failsafe. As we argued half to death in Section I, our Social Security benefits are relatively dependable and adjusted for inflation. Our savings are by nature inherently risky, and we want to know how it turns out if they don't do well other than to keep up their current value. If we do better in our actual retirement, that will be a happy worry. Our goal is to lay out plans that are reasonably bulletproof to the downside.

It turns out that the after-inflation-and-taxes returns on any savings have to be quite high in order to offset the benefits of waiting to claim our Social Security benefits later. How high? On the order of 5% to 7% real rate of return (return after inflation). That's every year. (We'll take a closer look at this later.) This depends also on how long we live: The longer we live the higher the rate of return needs to be. We believe strongly that we don't want to gamble the guaranteed benefits of waiting later to claim against the uncertainty of expecting (or, worse yet, depending on) high rates of return over decades of time. This is especially true if we have limited savings to begin with. Otherwise we run the risk of waking up in our 80s stuck in a minimal Social Security benefit with no savings left. That's no way to spend our later years.

And if we are among the fortunate who start with substantial amounts of savings, Financial Planning 101 tells us to diversify those assets and move them to less risky asset classes as we age. The best "less risky" asset to move to is to claim our Social Security benefits when they have reached their maximum value.

So if at all possible wait to claim no matter what.

➢ All numbers are in constant 2017 dollars.

➢ Tax is calculated for IRS returns with standard deduction and exemptions and 2017 brackets plus adjustment for the taxable portion of Social Security benefits if any. Assume the net gain on the sale of a principal residence when moving is tax-free (under $250,000 single and $500,000 married exemption). No consideration is given for state taxes, although most states do not tax Social Security benefits at all.

➢ Withdrawals from retirement savings are in amounts intended to ensure available funds in the regular savings to cover spending; also, some retirement savings are sold at times when no tax will be due to avoid paying higher taxes later.

➢ Required minimum distributions are applied to any tax-deferred retirement savings as of age 70 (not 70.5 as per IRS rule).

Onward to the first case.

CHAPTER 12

Gaby Part I: A Single Woman Starts to Live Her Dream

Has Some Savings and Starts at Age 62

Case 1-A: Gaby Moves at 62			
Current Age:	62		
Social Security Benefit At Age:	62	66	70
Benefit Amount Monthly	$1,350	$1,800	$2,376
Benefit Amount Annually	$16,200	$21,600	$28,512
Monthly Spending Budget: All-In	$1,500		$2,000
Annual Spending Budget: All-In	$18,000		$24,000
Relocation Spending	$10,000		
Retirement Account Savings	$125,000		
Regular Savings	$25,000		
Home Sale Net Proceeds	$50,000		
Total Savings Available	$200,000		

Gaby is longing for a big change. After 30 years in accounting for various small companies in Iowa, she is over it. During her career she enjoyed vacationing outside the U.S. in various places, though as she grew older she found she kept coming back to the beaches of the Caribbean. Now she is forming a plan to retire there. She wonders how much longer she will have to work before she can make her move…

Gaby found a perfect town on the beach where she looked carefully into housing and other living costs. About $10,000 should be plenty for her move: the trip down, ship a few belongings beyond what she carries in her suitcases, cover her apartment deposit as well as the cost of a residence visa. She is confident she can comfortably cover her living expenses for around $1,200 a month, including a cozy one-bedroom apartment that looks out to the water. Another $300 can cover her medical costs and minor contingencies. All told, $1,500 a month will support a delightful lifestyle, although she wants to plan to increase her monthly spending from $1,500 to about $2,000 around age 70 and indulge in a few more of life's luxuries as she gets older—but before she is too old to enjoy them.

Gaby has $125,000 in her IRA and $25,000 in a savings account— her emergency money. She also has a condo. She still owes some money on it but figures she would net about $50,000 from selling it after realtor and other expenses. All together she will have $200,000 available to fund the rest of her life, although she may have to pay income tax when she takes the money out of the IRA.

At Gaby's Full Retirement Age (66) she is eligible to receive a Social Security benefit in the amount of $1,800. (This is roughly the work-based benefit that someone who typically earned around $54,000 a year in to-day's dollars during their working career would be eligible to receive.) At 62 the benefit is reduced 25% to $1,350 for early claiming; wait to age 70 and the amount is increased by 32% for deferred retirement credits to $2,376.

Can she afford to make the move? She could start her Social Security right away: At $1,350 a month she would hardly need to touch her savings at all. But when she turns 70 she would have to dip into her savings each year by nearly $8,000 in order to spend the planned $2,000. Or she could wait to claim later when her benefits could be as high as $2,376 a month at age 70. That would cover even $2,000 a month of spending. In the meantime, though, spending $1,500 a month would burn through nearly all her saving in the eight years remaining until she turns 70 and starts her maximum benefit. Is it prudent to draw down so much of her savings?

Gaby's head starts to spin with all the options to consider…and she's an accountant. What to do…

Gaby's desire to avoid another dreary winter in Iowa is stronger than any obstacle so she sets out to analyze her options. She works on Plan A, in which she starts her Social Security benefits immediately, at 62, supplementing her living expenses from her other savings as needed. At 70 she ups her spending to $2,000, which draws somewhat more out of her savings. She also has to make minimum required distributions from her IRA, starting at around $4,500 for the year. However, she owes no income tax on these distributions. In fact, she takes another $2,500 out each year for good measure, moving the surplus to her savings, still with no federal taxes. (This strategy allows her to maintain an adequate sum in her savings; that way, if an emergency occurs she is less likely to need to sell a huge chunk of her retirement savings at once, triggering a big tax bill.)

By the way, Gaby is pleasantly surprised to learn she owes no federal taxes. After all, at age 71, for instance, her income consists of $16,200 from Social Security, $4,450 for the required minimum distribution, plus the added $2,500 she takes out of the IRA. That's a total of $23,150 of income. Her standard deduction and exemptions add up to only $11,950. Why no tax on the difference?

Social Security benefits are subject to special tax rules. Our benefits are counted to the extent only that we exceed certain thresholds of other income. For Gaby that means none of her benefits are taxable. Most people don't pay any tax on their Social Security income. With a little planning, even folks with moderate amounts of other income can usually manage their financial affairs to avoid paying much, if any, tax on their benefits.

Getting back to Gaby's Plan A, she is troubled to find that as she gets older her savings steadily dwindle. If she lives too long she is at risk of running out, forced to live solely on her Social Security benefits of $1,350 a month. That is not a comforting thought…

Gaby switches to work on Plan B, waiting to claim her benefits at age 70. She needs to draw substantially from her retirement accounts to bridge the gap between 62 and 70. In order to minimize income taxes she starts by withdrawing about $10,000 yearly from her IRA; at 65 she bumps this to $11,000 because she is eligible for an extra exemption (for being 65 and older, it pays to be a senior). Over the eight years of substantial IRA withdrawals taken to cover her expenses, she still avoids paying any federal income tax—not bad at all! At 70 she has about $46,000 remaining in her combined IRA and savings. She can now start collecting $2,376 a month from Social Security, and she ups her spending to $2,000, the same as Plan A. The extra $376 ($4,512 per year) goes to savings. Even at nearly $30,000 in combined Social Security benefits and required minimum distributions from her remaining IRA, she still owes no federal income taxes.

Gaby sits down to compare her two plans and see just how she does over time by comparing key milestones as she grows older. The outcomes are summarized in the table below:

Gaby's Savings at Key Age Milestones					
Gaby at Age:	**62**	**70**	**81**	**86**	**91**
Plan A: Claim Social Security at 62					
Retirement Account Savings	$125,000	$125,000	$54,200	$28,500	$8,300
Regular Savings*	$75,000	$50,600	$35,600	$22,300	$3,500
Total Savings	$200,000	$175,600	$89,800	$50,800	$11,800
Plan B: Claim Social Security at 70					
Retirement Account Savings	$125,000	$40,000	$24,300	$17,700	$11,700
Regular Savings*	$75,000	$6,000	$71,300	$100,500	$129,000
Total Savings	$200,000	$46,000	$95,600	$118,200	$140,700
*Includes $25,000 originally in savings plus $50,000 from net proceeds from sale of her condo.					

Starting with $200,000 in both plans at age 62, under Plan B Gaby has spent over 75% of her savings by age 70, versus barely over 10% if she claims early under Plan A. So far Plan A looks pretty good. Yet what's the worst outcome at this point for Plan B? If Gaby passes away she leaves a lot less money to…whom or what? If that's an important consideration, then so be it. She will have to decide accordingly. However, this is a financial plan for Gaby's life, not for after her death. And so far she has been living her dream, spending $1,500 a month under either plan in her Caribbean paradise. If she has a major financial emergency at age 70 she still has about $46,000 available to her: plenty for most contingencies she is likely to face at that point.

More importantly she now enjoys positive cash flow: $2,376 in Social Security income versus $2,000 in (increased) monthly spending. The good life is even better, and that extra income starts to add up. In fact, at some point shortly before she turns 81 her Plan B savings have pulled ahead of her Plan A savings—never mind that her Plan A savings are steadily shrinking while her Plan B savings are growing.

At age 86 Gaby has $118,000 under Plan B versus only $51,000 left under Plan A, a $67,000 difference that keeps growing. In other words, if Gaby lives to her average life expectancy—which is 86 for a female who reaches age 62—she is substantially ahead. One in four women who reach age 62 will live to age 91; if Gaby is among them, she will be $129,000 ahead. Under Plan B she is well positioned to deal with most financial hardships she might face at a time in life when she has no reasonable options to deal with problems except to slash her spending.

Under Plan A she will run out of savings in another year or two and have to cut spending to her $1,350 per month Social Security benefit… and hope she doesn't run into an emergency. Financial worry is all but guaranteed as she ages.

Let's recap. Both plans have identical spending in Gaby's Caribbean paradise. Plan A claims Social Security early to preserve other savings but runs out of those savings if Gaby lives a long time. Plan B draws down the savings early in order to claim Social Security benefits later when they have grown 76% in value. If Gaby passes away in her early 70s, she will leave less money behind for…someone. However, if Gaby lives only to her average life expectancy she is $67,000 ahead and becoming more and more financially secure as she ages. Her finances are growing.

Here's another way to look at Gaby's options over time by presenting her combined savings at the end of each year in side-by-side charts for each claiming scenario:

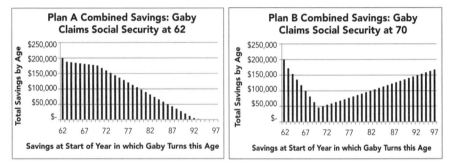

Claiming at 62 delivers steadily declining financial security over the years. Claiming at 70 shows declining savings the first 8 years, then steadily improving financial security over the years.

Gaby weighs the risk of having a bit less to leave behind if she dies in her early 70s (very unlikely) versus the risk of spending her later years on a fixed income worried about money all the time. Hmmmm… We are not surprised to learn that Gaby picks Plan B.

"Yeah, but…" we hear you cry. "Surely Gaby can do much better on Plan A if she wisely invests her savings while living off her Social Security benefits." We will look at this shortly. First, however, what if Gaby is 60 instead of 62? Must she wait to 62 to split for the Caribbean? Endure two more winters in Iowa? Or is there a way for her to bail out of there now and still make it all work? Stay tuned…

Key Takeaways

The option to claim our Social Security benefits at age 62 versus age 70 usually offers a choice of trade-offs. The trade-off for claiming early: If we die early—usually in our 70s—we will leave relatively more money behind for our heirs or whoever gets the extra money; if we live into our 80s we have less guaranteed money each month, and that could pinch our finances when we are too old to do anything about it.

The trade-off for claiming later: If we die early, we leave less money for our heirs. The problem is that we probably won't die early; if we don't, we collect more and more money. Our monthly check is 76% more than our age 62 check. If we live to the average life expectancy we have more money to leave our heirs. If we just keep on living and living there is more and more money to either spend or leave the heirs. From this point of view, the choice seems obvious: Claim at 70.

CHAPTER 13

Gaby Part II: A Single Woman Starts to Live Her Dream—Even Earlier

Has Savings and Starts at Age 60

Case 1-B: Gaby Moves at 60 Instead of 62				
Current Age:	60			
Social Security Benefit At Age:		62	66	70
Benefit Amount Monthly		$1,350	$1,800	$2,376
Benefit Amount Annually		$16,200	$21,600	$28,512
Monthly Spending Budget: All-In	$1,500			$2,000
Annual Spending Budget: All-In	$18,000			$24,000
Relocation Spending	$10,000			
Retirement Account Savings	$125,000			
Regular Savings	$25,000			
Home Sale Net Proceeds	$50,000			
Total Savings Available	$200,000			

We are wondering if Gaby can leave her job in Iowa and make her move to the Caribbean when she is 60, instead of waiting to age 62. Her spending plan is otherwise identical to what it was before, and her total savings and net proceeds from the sale of her home are also the same. Her Social Security benefits are also identical in this example.

As before, Gaby runs the numbers. In both plans she will have to live off her savings between 60 and 62; then in Plan A she claims her benefits at 62, while in Plan B she waits to age 70.

We recall from the prior case in which Gaby starts her adventure at age 62 that she saw that under Plan A she was running out of savings in her early 90s. Not surprisingly, as we see in the table below, starting two years early with no initial source of outside income only makes her run out of savings earlier, shortly before she turns 87. Thereafter she would have to get by on her monthly age-62 benefit of $1,350. Note that age 87 is only one year past her average life expectancy, so there's a good chance she will live to encounter this problem.

What about Plan B? By drawing on her savings two years earlier she takes an additional $36,000 out of her savings before she turns 70. (That's $1,500 per month x 12 months x 2 years.) As a result, instead of around $46,000 left in her savings at age 70, she has only about $9,000. However, from then on she is collecting her maximized Social Security check and her savings begin to rebuild.

The summary results are presented in the table below.

Gaby Moves at Age 60 Instead of 62 Her Savings at Key Age Milestones					
Gaby at Age:	60	70	81	86	91
Plan A: Claim Social Security at 62					
Retirement Account Savings	$125,000	$125,000	$36,800	$7,000	$0
Regular Savings*	$75,000	$14,600	$17,000	$7,800	$0
Total Savings	$200,000	$139,600	$53,800	$14,800	$0
Plan B: Claim Social Security at 70					
Retirement Account Savings	$125,000	$6,300	$3,800	$2,800	$1,800
Regular Savings*	$75,000	$3,000	$55,100	$78,700	$102,200
Total Savings	$200,000	$9,300	$58,900	$81,500	$104,000

*Includes $25,000 originally in savings plus $50,000 from net proceeds from sale of her condo.

Let's begin by focusing on the age-70 remaining savings. Clearly, Plan B is cutting it tight, to say the least. With only $7,000 left in savings there is little surplus available for an emergency at age 70. But let's dig a bit deeper into the Social Security rules because they offer useful insights into some of the options that come available to those who wait to claim their benefits.

First, Gaby always has the option to start her benefits. Every month after age 62. If she starts to worry too much about the near term and she can find no alternative, she can file.

Here's another neat trick: Up until age 70 she can make her claim retroactive up to six months and receive a tidy lump sum payment followed by a regular monthly payment.

Consider an example. Suppose Gaby has a financial mishap around age 69. She can simply decide to start her benefits a little earlier than she originally planned. At that age it would be $2,232, still more than the $2,000 she wants to begin spending at age 70. Or she could file a six-month retroactive claim. In that case her benefit would be smaller—as if she had filed it at age 68 and six months: $2,160 per month. The lump sum would be six times this amount: $12,960! Together with her remaining savings and her increased monthly benefit, that might well be more than enough to tide her through her rough patch. It's nice to have options.

That said, once Gaby files at age 70 she is locked in going forward. She wants to be reasonably confident that her remaining savings can probably tide her over for the near term while her savings begin to rebuild. Still, any way you cut it, Gaby is likely to be far better off waiting to claim at 70 than at 62, even if she bails on Iowa and her job at age 60 to start her dream earlier.

The charts on the next page reflect these two plans for Gaby starting her adventure at age 60 instead of 62. The Plan A chart illustrates the steady and rapid decline in savings for Gaby until running out in her mid-80s. Plan B shows the rapid decline to age 70 with growing savings thereafter.

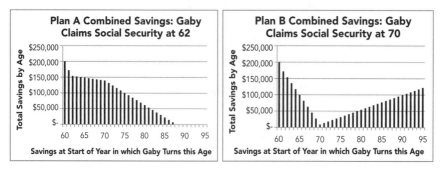

Not surprisingly Gaby is far more comfortable with Plan B, especially knowing she can start her Social Security benefit with a six-month retroactive claim if she gets into a bind.

Key Takeaways

Another trade-off we often face is the number of years between the age we first make our move overseas and age 70. We can add to these years by moving earlier if we are willing to dig deeper into our savings, as illustrated in this case. Of course, another alternative to reach the same goal of leaving earlier would be to lower the monthly spending budget until age 70. Or we might be able to find some income during those years to offset our expenses. Finally, we can always claim our benefits a bit earlier if we need to.

Life is full of trade-offs. We want to make ours when we clearly and fully understand what the costs and benefits of the alternatives are.

CHAPTER 14
Gaby Part III: Fixing a Broken Claiming Strategy
Gaby Starts at Age 62, Suspends at 66, Restarts at 70

Plus the "Problem" of Happy Worries: When Returns Exceed Expectations

In this chapter we will consider the case of all those Gaby's out there reading this that already started their benefits at or around age 62 and are wondering if there is anything they can do to undo their decision. Do they have any options? We also want to take a look at that "Yeah but…" we raised back in Chapter 12: "What about investing all those savings so they do better than just keep up with inflation?" Fair question. We'll get to it. Hold on.

But first, back to the matter of repairing a broken claiming strategy. There are a couple of options. First, if you started less than one year ago, you can withdraw your claim for benefits and pay back any you received and start over. We covered this in Chapter 11.

Second, and also briefly covered in Chapter 11, if the withdrawal of claim is not an option, you can still exercise your right to stop receiving your benefits once or after you reach your Full Retirement Age (the Social Security Administration calls this "suspending your benefits"). You can resume collecting benefits anytime up to age 70.

How would this work for Gaby if she started out on Plan A? (We return here to the original Chapter 12 case in which she is 62 starting out, not 60.) She would suspend her benefits at age 66. Her monthly receipts of $1,350 would stop, and she would shift to living off her savings. Then, at age 70, she would resume receipt of her benefits, which would have grown 32%—$432 more per month—to $1,782 (plus any inflation over the last four years—remember that our benefits are increased each year for inflation, whether we have started them or not). The results are summarized in the table below:

Gaby Claims at 62, Suspends at 66, Resumes at 70 Savings at Key Age Milestones					
Gaby at Age:	**62**	**70**	**81**	**86**	**91**
Plan A: Claim Social Security at 62					
Retirement Account Savings	$125,000	$125,000	$54,200	$28,500	$8,300
Regular Savings*	$75,000	$50,600	$35,600	$22,300	$3,500
Total Savings	$200,000	$175,600	$89,800	$50,800	$11,800
Plan A — Suspend at 66: Reclaim Social Security at 70					
Retirement Account Savings	$125,000	$109,000	$66,300	$48,200	$32,000
Regular Savings*	$75,000	$1,800	$15,700	$20,700	$23,900
Total Savings	$200,000	$110,800	$82,000	$68,900	$55,900

*Includes $25,000 originally in savings plus $50,000 from net proceeds from sale of her condo.

Again, Gaby has not modified her lifestyle by one penny. All she has done is shift to spending from her savings while she waits for her Social Security benefit to grow from age 66, when she has the option to suspend her benefits, until age 70, when she resumes them. She is clearly better off than under the original Plan A scheme, with just over $44,000 more in remaining savings at age 91. In addition, her savings are only going down at the rate of $2,616 each year, compared with $7,800 a year under the original plan. If her spending continues without a severe emergency she will probably outlive her savings.

Following are the side-by-side charts for these two plans:

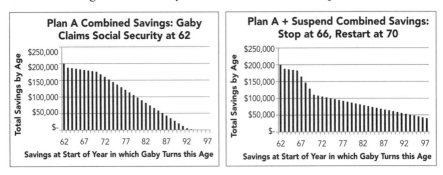

While neither plan provides for growing financial security as Gaby ages, it's clear which provides greater security. And, as we will see next, perhaps a little better luck with her investments over the years will be enough to deliver sufficient financial well-being.

Weighing the Impact of Average or Above-Average Rates of Return on Savings

OK, now we turn to the "Yeah, but…" "Finally," we hear you cry! Here's the crux of your question to me: "You are assuming that our retirement accounts and savings earn enough to only keep up with inflation—an unrealistically low rate of return. Won't reasonable earnings on our original savings more than make up for the shortfall from claiming our benefits early?"

Staying with the Chapter 12 base case in which Gaby begins her Caribbean life at age 62, what if she is able to generate a 5% rate of return on her savings over her retirement? (Recall that this is the real interest rate, before taking inflation into account, which would add 2% to 3% to this rate to bring it to nominal rates.) Here's how her savings would look over time at her key age milestones:

Gaby Earns 5% Rate of Return (before inflation) Savings at Key Age Milestones					
Gaby at Age:	**62**	**70**	**81**	**86**	**91**
Plan A: Claim Social Security at 62					
Retirement Account Savings	$125,000	$128,100	$136,300	$128,700	$111,400
Regular Savings*	$75,000	$119,400	$172,700	$218,600	$281,100
Total Savings	$200,000	$247,500	$309,000	$347,300	$392,500
Compare to 0% Return Total Savings (from earlier)	$200,000	$175,600	$89,800	$50,800	$11,800
Plan B: Claim Social Security at 70					
Retirement Account Savings	$125,000	$62,900	$67,100	$63,400	$54,900
Regular Savings*	$75,000	$31,100	$154,800	$241,700	$351,400
Total Savings	$200,000	$94,000	$221,900	$305,100	$406,300
Compare to 0% Return Total Savings (from earlier)	$200,000	$46,000	$95,600	$118,200	$129,000

*Includes $25,000 originally in savings plus $50,000 from net proceeds from sale of her condo.

What's going on behind these numbers? On balance Plan A leaves Gaby slightly better off than Plan B, at least until she is getting quite old. If we compare her finances at her life expectancy age (86), Plan A is about $42,000 ahead. Only if she lives to her one-in-four life expectancy does she come out ahead under Plan B. However, this misses the larger point: If this is the outcome it doesn't matter much which plan she chooses. Either way she ends up with considerably more money than she started with—and more than enough to move up to a considerably more expensive lifestyle if she chooses. Either plan offers multiple happy choices.

The problem is that we do not know the rates of return we will enjoy when we start out. Our mission is not to concern ourselves with "happy worries." If we find ourselves in that situation, we know that there are armies of "happy worry advisors" ready to help us manage and spend our extra "happy money" for a fee—which makes those advisors happy…

Instead, our mission is to worry about what could go wrong and hedge against that set of circumstances. To this end in the table above we have added the Plan A and Plan B results from the original scenario under which Gaby gets a 0% rate of return on her savings (except a rate sufficient to keep up with inflation). This line is called "Compare to 0% Return Total Savings (from earlier)" in the table. It is instructive to compare this line to the Total Savings line above it for each of Plans A and B.

Plan A looks a lot better with a 5% rate of return than with a 0% rate of return, about as good as Plan B in the long run. However, if those 5% returns don't materialize, Plan A has much bigger risks to the downside. In fact, Plan A can lead to Gaby running out of savings and being forced to live solely on her Social Security in her early 90s: a grim prospect if she is "unfortunate" enough to live too long.

Plan B does a much better job of hedging the downside risk or running out of money—it doesn't matter if the rate of return merely keeps up with inflation. Yet on the upside it is almost as good as Plan A. Either way, under Plan B Gaby probably ends up with more money than she needs and lives in "happy worry" land.

Indeed, if we keep increasing the rate of return the upside potential increases slightly with Plan A, compared with Plan B, although each plan just ends up with more and more money. The problem is that increasing the rate of return this way delivers an increasingly unlikely outcome—it's nice to fanaticize about, but it's probably not going to happen. Moreover, I never heard anyone express a (serious) worry about having too much money; I have heard plenty worry about not having enough.

Here are the side-by-side charts comparing Gaby's savings as she ages under the two different plans:

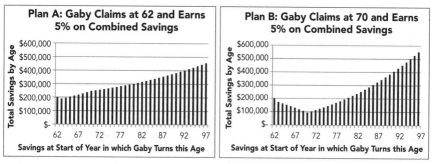

Plan B—waiting to claim at 70—provides powerful protection against poor performance in the market and running out of money. Gaby has made her decision. What about the rest of us?

Planning Rules for Social Security Claiming Success

From all of this we can begin to distill several simple planning rules that can serve us well, regardless of our starting point and circumstances:

➤ Find a way to claim later. Either wait to age 70 for a work-based claim or Full Retirement Age for a spousal claim. At the near-retirement stage of our lives, claiming later is the best guaranteed hedge we have against running out of money in our old age.

➤ Find a lifestyle in which our spending on essential needs does not exceed our benefits when we claim later. Once our benefits start, allocate a share to savings if our current financial situation does not provide a sufficient emergency cushion. To the extent we find too much money piling up, enjoy spending more on non-essentials.

➤ Find a way to finance our lives until we can claim our benefits later, whether from savings, work, a tighter budget, or any combination thereof.

Follow these simple guidelines and the risks of running out of money are relatively small.

And if savings and/or work result in an excess of money, we will never be at a loss for opportunities to spend it.

Key Takeaways

If we are already locked into an earlier claim age (claimed before we stumbled onto this book…), we can still take one step to remedy the situation. Assuming our FRA is 66 we can suspend receipt of our benefits at that age. We won't be receiving any benefits for the next four years, so we need income or savings to live on. At age 70, however, we can resume our benefits and they will be 32% greater (plus the interim inflation during those years of suspension). Note that your spouse cannot collect a spouse claim during the years that you suspend until you resume collecting your benefit.

All our cases (except this last one) assume zero real return on our savings and investments. This is conservative (although returns can be negative, as we experienced so vividly during the Great Recession). Our view is we want to plan for a poor investment future and still be comfortable with income sufficient to be financially secure as we age. However, we see in this case that even with decent returns, Plan B—waiting to claim later—does almost as well as Plan A—claiming early. Plan B hedges the downside risks without giving up much of the upside potential.

And if our finances turn out better—as they probably will—we will call this a happy worry and leave the extra money for you to deal with on your own. We are sure you will be up to the task.

CHAPTER 15

Alison and Marcus: A Vacation Visit Leads to a Change in Plans

Informed Trade-offs: When it can Make Sense to Claim Benefits Earlier

It's January, and 62-year-olds Alison and Marcus are enjoying an enchanting trip to see their friends Marilyn and Jason who live in the city of David in Panama. A few days into their stay Alison observes over dinner, "Marcus and I can't imagine ever being able to afford to live like this!"

Jason looks back at them quizzically: "It probably costs a lot less than you think. Don't get me wrong; we feel like we're living the high life—and we are. We just don't have the big bills you might expect if you are living in the States."

Marilyn adds, "We don't even pay close attention to our expenses anymore because we no longer worry about them; when we first moved here, though, I worried about them and tracked them all the time. We never spent over $2,000 a month, and I am sure that is still true. That includes rent for our place, food, local travel and entertainment, healthcare, everything—add a bit extra for a trip back to the States once or twice a year. That's it."

Alison and Marcus look at one another in disbelief. The next morning they set out on their own with a purpose: to look into rental properties and check out expenses in the market. It doesn't take them long to realize that, indeed, $2,000 could take them very far in this town. Just like that, a vacation trip to visit friends in an exotic location turns into a window of possibility. Perhaps they are not doomed to many more years of toil before they can realize their dreams for the next phase of their lives. Work is fine, but they have been there, done that…

Upon their return to snowy New Hampshire, Alison and Marcus set out to collect all their numbers to try to figure out if they can make a move sooner rather than later. They look up their Social Security benefits (which are listed for various claim ages in the table below), along with other particulars of their plan. They talk to their real estate agent and are bummed out to learn that they will probably lose about $12,000 when they sell their house—they bought it in 2006, with values at a peak. But they guess they are lucky not to lose more. After the house sale they will be left with about $55,000 in savings and another $120,000 in their retirement accounts.

Based on their own research, along with the testimony of Marilyn and Jason, they are convinced that they can live more than comfortably on $2,500 a month once they relocate. They would also like to know if they can bump that up a bit, to $3,000 a month when they reach 70. Maybe they won't, but it would be comforting to know they can if they want or need to.

Case 2: Alison and Marcus Move at 62			
Current Age:	62		
Social Security Benefit At Age:	62	66	70
Benefit Monthly – Alison	$1,350	$1,800	$2,376
Benefit Monthly – Marcus	$1,125	$1,500	$1,980
Benefit Amount Monthly	$2,475	$3,300	$4,356
Benefit Amount Annually	$29,700	$39,600	$52,272
Monthly Spending Budget: All-In	$2,500		$3,000
Annual Spending Budget: All-In	$30,000		$36,000
Relocation Spending	$15,000		
Retirement Account Savings	$120,000		
Regular Savings	$67,000		
Home Sale Net Proceeds	-$12,000		
Total Savings Available	$175,000		

In a Skype call Marilyn reminds them to allow for relocation expenses. They conclude that $15,000 should be sufficient. However, with the dent in savings caused by the loss on the sale of the house, can they still afford to leave the rat race behind and retire to Panama?

If they both start their Social Security benefits now at age 62 (Plan A), they'll receive $2,475 a month combined. That's almost enough to cover the initial monthly budget of $2,500 without touching much of their savings. However, can they afford to up the spending to $3,000 a month when they reach 70? That would dig into their savings at the rate of around $6,000 a year (assuming a return on savings that just keeps up with inflation). Would their savings last?

On the other hand, if they could only wait to age 70 to claim Social Security they would collect $4,356 a month. That amount is way more than enough to cover their increased spending of $3,000 at that age and still save around $1,356 monthly to replenish the savings they would need to spend before 70. But do they have enough savings? The math says "No." If they move and start spending $2,500 a month, that's $30,000 a year for eight years to age 70. They need $240,000 and have only $160,000 left after relocation expenses of about $15,000. This plan doesn't work.

Should they work a few more years until they are closer to age 70 to make it work? After getting their hopes up, the prospect of more years at the grind is, frankly, sickening. Marcus suggests that they could claim early and hope for the best in the long run. Alison, ever the practical one, reminds Marcus that "Hope is not a plan…"

Married couples have so many options… When we run the numbers it turns out that if Marcus starts his benefit earlier, at age 64, it is reduced from his FRA amount of $1,500 to $1,300. With this plan Marcus's benefit, combined with remaining savings, is just enough to get them to age 70, when Alison can claim her maximized benefit in the amount of $2,376. Their combined benefit is $3,676, and they have also maximized the survivor benefit based on Alison's higher starting benefit level. Always wise… They have found a viable Plan B. (It is a further comfort to know that they can always shift Marcus's benefit start date depending on how their spending goes: earlier if they run short of savings and later if lower spending or higher return on their investments allow.)

The table below shows the remaining savings at various ages under the two plans:

Alison & Marcus' Savings at Key Age Milestones					
Alison & Marcus at Age:	62	70	80	86	91
Plan A: Both Claim Social Security at 62					
Retirement Account Savings	$120,000	$120,000	$56,700	$26,300	$6,800
Regular Savings*	$55,000	$37,600	$37,900	$30,500	$18,500
Total Savings	$175,000	$157,600	$94,600	$56,800	$25,300
Plan B: Marcus Claims Social Security at 64; Alison Claims at 70					
Retirement Account Savings	$120,000	$10,000	$6,400	$4,400	$2,900
Regular Savings*	$55,000	$3,200	$87,900	$138,600	$180,700
Total Savings	$175,000	$13,200	$94,300	$142,000	$183,600
*Includes $67,000 originally in savings less $12,000 net loss from sale of their home.					

Just as they had suspected, their savings are being drained dangerously low under Plan A, in which they both claim at age 62. At Alison's average life expectancy of 86 they have only $56,800 remaining; under Plan B at that same age they have $142,000 in savings that are growing a bit over $8,000 a year. Their nest egg under Plan B gets more and more secure.

To be sure, Plan B draws their savings down as they approach age 70 with only $13,200 remaining at that time versus $157,600 remaining under Plan A. However, they hold the same options Gaby held as Alison nears age 70: File for her benefits a little earlier and/or file a six-month retroactive claim to get a quick lump sum if there is a sudden need. Again, once they reach age 70 and Alison starts collecting, the lump sum option goes away. Their savings replenish fairly quickly. Around age 80 they have almost as much in savings remaining under either plan, though Plan A's savings are steadily falling while Plan B's steadily rising.

Either plan gets them out of New Hampshire right now. Yet look at all Plan B offers, compared with Plan A: (1) the exact same spending of $2,500 at 62 and $3,000 beginning at age 70; (2) $3,676 versus $2,475 in monthly income once they reach age 70, $14,412 more per year, extra money to save or spend as they see fit; and (3) a survivor benefit of $2,376 versus only $1,485 under Plan A—$10,692 more per year in financial security for the survivor.

Following are the side-by-side comparison charts for these two plans:

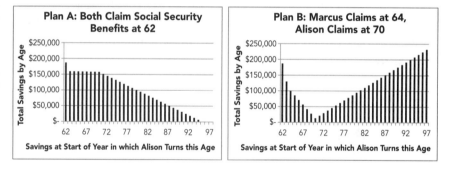

Note that while your author has been harping at you incessantly about everyone waiting to age 70 (or Full Retirement Age for a spousal claim) to claim, here's an instance in which Marcus claims early, at 64. How can this be?

Life is all about trade-offs. The question is whether we have enough information to make well-informed decisions concerning our choices. Most people are clueless about all the ways in which their Social Security benefits can be tapped in the context of a larger financial plan to support a dream life. Fortunately, Alison and Marcus have the information they need—their benefits at various ages and their starting savings—to evaluate their trade-offs. They conclude that a plan that lets them move now and that supports a more-than-comfortable budget past age 70 with ever-growing savings thereafter gets them what they want now while affording greater financial security as they get older. Moreover, they know that they have room to cut spending a bit if need be: They already did their spending due diligence while they visited Marilyn and Jason. And if their savings outperform "just keeping up with inflation"? Happy worries! They go with Plan B.

Key Takeaways

In some cases it can best serve our overall interests for one spouse to claim earlier, as in this case. In general, we lean toward doing whatever is necessary to start the dream sooner rather than later. This can mean lowering the monthly spending (at least to age 70) or finding some other income. In this case, a roomier spending budget now requires one spouse to claim earlier, at age 64. Our couple finds that this affords them a better lifestyle currently while still permitting their savings to rebound adequately starting at age 70. Moreover, they are still able to lock in the maximum survivor benefit—critically important for long-run financial security when other savings are limited.

CHAPTER 16
Simon and Michelle: She Wants to Volunteer Closer to the Action
A Work-Record Claim Coupled with a Spouse Claim

We have been considering situations that involve benefits solely based on our work records. What if we are married and one spouse has little or no work record? As we saw much earlier, said spouse at FRA is eligible to receive 50% of the amount that the working spouse is eligible to receive at their FRA. That's called a spouse benefit. There is no point in delaying beyond FRA to claim it, since the amount doesn't increase as it does for a work-based benefit; however, the amount is reduced if the spouse benefit is claimed before FRA. If claimed at 62, for instance, it is reduced from 50% to 35% of the working spouse's FRA benefit.

Consider the case of Simon and Michelle. While Simon's career has been OK, he is ready for a change. Michelle has kept more than busy with a host of volunteer positions; she now serves on a number of boards for non-profit organizations. She cherishes her non-profit work. She brings Simon along on a trip organized by the Rotary through Central America focused on providing extra classroom supplies to primary school children. She is drawn to the possibility of volunteer work overseas that brings her closer to the actual recipients. Simon says, "I'm ready—sign me up too!" They want to see if they can afford to pull this off.

Case 3: Simon and Michelle			
Current Ages: Simon – 62 and Michelle – 60			
Social Security Benefit At Age:	62	66	70
Benefit Monthly – Simon	$1,350	$1,800	$2,376
Benefit Monthly – Michelle*	$630	$900	$900
Benefit Amount Monthly	$1,985	$2,700	$3,276
Benefit Amount Annually	$23,820	$32,400	$39,312
Monthly Spending Budget: All-In	$1,700		$2,500
Annual Spending Budget: All-In	$20,400		$30,000
Relocation Spending	$12,000		
Retirement Account Savings	$125,000		
Regular Savings	$30,000		
Home Sale Net Proceeds	$25,000		
Total Savings Available	$180,000		
*Michelle cannot start her spouse benefit unless Simon has started to collect his; see below for exceptions			

As if Social Security isn't already complicated enough, we introduce an age difference for Case 3: Simon is 62 and Michelle is 60. His FRA benefit is $1,800. Though Michelle worked little during her adulthood, she is still eligible for a spouse benefit based on Simon's work record: when she is 66 she can collect 50% of what he could collect at his FRA. However, under the new rules enacted by the Bipartisan Budget Act of 2015, she cannot collect a spouse benefit unless he has started to collect his work-based benefit. (If Simon was at least 66 by April 29, 2016, and he filed for and suspended receipt of his benefits before that date, then Michelle can collect the spouse benefit at age 66. See Chapter 10 for more details.)

As shown in the table above for Case 3, they have $125,000 in retirement account savings and will have $55,000 in their regular savings once they sell their house and put the net proceeds into that account.

They plan on an initial spending budget of $1,700 a month and intend to increase that almost 50%, to $2,500, when he reaches age 70 (she'll be 68). From what they have learned, $1,700 will be quite comfortable for now, and $2,500 later will allow them to indulge in more travel and household help.

Continuing our comparisons of savings at key ages as we did in previous cases, the table below presents the total savings at various ages for Simon. Bear in mind that Michelle is two years younger at each of these milestones.

Simon & Michelle's Savings at Key Age Milestones					
When Simon is Age:	**62**	**70**	**81**	**86**	**91**
Plan A: Both Claim Social Security at 62					
Retirement Account Savings	$125,000	$125,000	$54,200	$28,500	$8,300
Regular Savings*	$55,000	$54,800	$56,900	$51,400	$40,400
Total Savings	$180,000	$179,800	$111,100	$79,900	$48,700
Plan B: Simon Claims at 70; Michelle Claims at 68					
Retirement Account Savings	$125,000	$4,000	$2,400	$1,800	$1,200
Regular Savings*	$55,000	$800	$104,800	$152,000	$199,200
Total Savings	$180,000	$4,800	$107,200	$153,800	$200,400
*Includes $30,000 originally in savings plus $25,000 net gain from sale of their home.					

Under Plan A they move now and Simon, who is 62, starts his age-62 benefit of $1,350. That doesn't quite cover their monthly budget of $1,700, so they dip into savings for the difference until Michelle turns 62 two years later. She receives $630 a month for a spouse benefit that is 50% of what Simon would have received at age 66, reduced 30% for her claiming it at 62 instead of 66. Together they now receive $1,980 a month, enough to cover the budget and add $280 back into savings.

When Simon is 70 (Michelle is 68) they switch to spending $2,500 per month and start dipping back into savings to make up the difference. As a result, their savings are steadily dwindling as they get older, and there is steadily increasing risk of running out of money if they live too long or have an emergency.

Under Plan B Simon waits to claim at age 70 in the amount of $2,376. Michelle cannot start her spouse benefit until Simon starts his under the new rules that apply to anyone who turns 66 after April 29, 2016. Under the old rules—see Chapter 10—Simon could have filed for benefits at age 66 and then suspended receipt of those benefits. This allowed him to wait to 70 to get the higher benefit while it entered him into the system so that his spouse could collect a spouse benefit.

There is some speculation that this outcome was unintended by the legislators because it creates a somewhat perverse outcome: Simon could start his benefit at 68 when it would be $2,088, or $288 less per month ($3,456 per year). Then Michelle could start her spouse benefit at age 66 in the full amount of $900. In other words, by claiming early they give up $3,456 per year thereafter in exchange for receiving two more years at $900 a month, or $21,600.

That's a tempting though bad deal. By waiting to claim they recoup the difference in less than seven years, when Simon is 75 and Michelle is 73. Moreover, they get locked into a lower survivor benefit. Giving up that extra $288 a month could be very important to the survivor.

When Congress changed this rule in 2015 it intended to prevent a different claiming strategy than this one. As the problem introduced by this new law becomes increasingly evident it may be the case that corrective legislation will be introduced. We want to watch for a possible change to this in the coming years if the situation described herein applies to us.

Getting back to Plan B with Simon and Michelle claiming when he turns 70, their combined benefit is $3,276. While their savings have dwindled to just under $5,000 at that point, from then on they begin to be replenished at the rate of $9,312 a year. The savings in each plan are about equal when he turns 81 (Michelle is 79); by the time Simon is 86 (about a year after his average life expectancy—she is still two years from hers) their Plan B savings are about $154,000, almost $74,000 greater than Plan A and growing stronger every month.

The side-by-side chart comparison reflects these outcomes over the years:

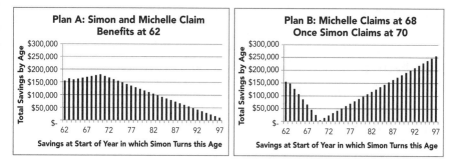

Even though the savings appear to dip so close to zero in the Plan B chart, keep in mind that Simon could always start his benefit a bit earlier if it becomes a problem. While that's not best for the survivor benefit, it is a comfort for them to know that the option is available should they need to claim slightly before 70.

As presented, the survivor benefit is $2,376 under Plan B; Plan A is only $1,485, $891 less per month ($10,692 per year). That's 60% more income for the survivor under Plan B. Just imagine what a difference that could make as we age. Suppose Simon passes away when he is 86. Under Plan A Michelle receives $1,485 a month and has only about $80,000 in remaining savings. She will have to slash her spending from the $2,500 level; otherwise she will run out of her savings when she is 90 or so. What kind of life is that for an elderly person?

By contrast, under Plan B Michelle collects $2,376 a month and has $154,000 in the bank. With Simon gone she probably won't need to spend $2,500 each month. In sum she can continue both a high standard of living along with regular contributions to her savings so that as she ages—in comfort—her financial security keeps growing. That's what Simon would wish for his wife—as she would for herself.

Key Takeaways

A spouse waiting to file a work-based claim at 70 can prevent the other spouse from collecting a spouse benefit until then. That forces a trade-off that can be costly (the spouse benefits are foregone while waiting), yet it usually still pays before very long—never mind the importance of the worker spouse waiting anyway to maximize the survivor benefit. In this instance, where he is two years older, the trade-off is tolerable and the decision is clear. It gets less clear to the extent the ages differ. We just have to figure out how to make our spending budget work until the worker spouse reaches 70.

CHAPTER 17

Becky and Tony: Out of Financial Catastrophe to a Brighter Future

Two Work-Based Claims—No Savings

Becky and Tony played it by the book. With solid careers for both, they bought a home where they raised two children, saving diligently for college and retirement.

An earlier trip to the Galapagos Islands of Ecuador included time to explore the country's capital, Quito, and some of the surrounding cities. They left enchanted, promising this would be the place where they would retire one day.

The kids finished school, and they turned to thoughts of retirement… Then disaster struck in the form of a malicious lawsuit. As their legal fees soared, eating into their savings, they were forced to liquidate nearly everything in order to settle. They even lost their home.

As the dust settled from the legal calamity, they found themselves still employed but starting out anew to build their savings from scratch. Becky and Tony are 62 and depressed about their situation. They had always enjoyed a decent standard of living, and the prospect of living frugally and working many years to save up some degree of financial security for their old age was daunting.

What else could they do? It was either work well into their later years or try to limp by on Social Security. That couldn't provide a decent life… Could it?

One night Tony tries to leave their worries behind by looking up some of the places they had visited in Ecuador, including Cotacachi.

A search turns up an article on *International Living's* website. He reads about avocados at three for a dollar and starts to wonder if they might not be able to start over somewhere affordable yet comfortable. Maybe they could salvage a better life now from the recent disaster. Tony dug up some more information and shared it with Becky. Could there be some sunshine around the corner after all?

Tony and Becky learn that they can live quite decently in Cotacachi on $1,500 a month. They are in complete agreement that they want to live within a budget that will eventually let them rebuild some savings. With accrued vacation from when they quit their jobs, they have enough cash remaining (about $10,000) to relocate and get their visas. What are their options if they decide to make this leap relying solely on their Social Security benefits? Is there a dream yet to be lived in their lives?

They can file for Social Security benefits—the same amount for each—in the amounts listed in the table below for various claim ages:

Case 4: Tony and Becky Move at 62			
Current Age:	62		
Social Security Benefit At Age:	62	66	70
Benefit Monthly – Tony	$1,500	$2,000	$2,640
Benefit Monthly – Becky	$1,500	$2,000	$2,640
Benefit Amount Monthly	$3,000	$4,000	$5,280
Benefit Amount Annually	$36,000	$48,000	$63,360
Monthly Spending Budget: All-In	$1,500		$3,500
Annual Spending Budget: All-In	$18,000		$42,000
Relocation Spending	$10,000		
Retirement Account Savings	$ 0		
Regular Savings	$10,000		
Home Sale Net Proceeds	$ 0		
Total Savings Available	$10,000		

They are surprised to see just how far their benefits can take them, regardless of age. Clearly, they can afford a starter budget of $1,500 a month. They wonder if they can up that to a luxurious $3,500 a month at age 70… Maybe it's not too late to live a dream…

In the table below we compare alternatives much as before: Under Plan A both Tony and Becky claim their benefits at age 62, and under Plan B only Tony starts his benefit while Becky waits to claim hers at age 70.

Tony & Becky's Savings at Key Age Milestones					
Tony & Becky at Age:	**62**	**70**	**81**	**86**	**91**
Plan A: Both Claim Social Security at 62					
Retirement Account Savings	$ 0	$ 0	$ 0	$ 0	$ 0
Regular Savings*	$10,000	$144,000	$78,000	$48,000	$18,000
Total Savings	$10,000	$144,000	$78,000	$48,000	$18,000
Plan B: Tony Claims Social Security at 62; Becky Claims at 70					
Retirement Account Savings	$ 0	$ 0	$ 0	$ 0	$ 0
Regular Savings*	$10,000	$ 0	$84,500	$122,900	$161,300
Total Savings	$10,000	$ 0	$84,500	$122,900	$161,300
*Just enough to cover their relocation expenses.					

The usual pattern appears: If both claim at 62 (Plan A) they can spend one benefit and save the other beginning immediately. In Plan B, by contrast, they claim only one benefit, waiting to age 70 to claim the larger benefit. Only then do they begin to build any savings. As in our previous cases, Plan A offers maximum savings at age 70; afterwards the savings decline because the benefits of $3,000 a month are less than the new spending plan of $3,500.

Plan B starts with only Tony's check at 62 to live on; there are no savings at age 70. Thereafter, however, the savings build rapidly because the combined benefit beginning at age 70 is $4,140: That's $640 more per month than the $3,500 revised spending plan. By Becky's average life expectancy they are considerably ahead under Plan B. In fact, they were ahead shortly before Becky's 81st birthday, with their financial security growing each month thereafter.

You can follow the pattern over the years in the side-by-side chart comparison:

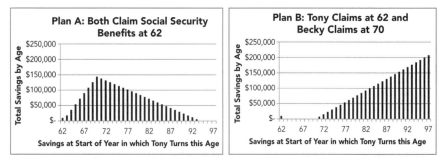

Either plan probably beats going back to work in New Hampshire to try to rebuild their former life. Each plan offers opportunities to rebuild their savings. And let's get real for a moment: $3,500 a month is an exceedingly generous amount for a couple to live on almost anywhere in the world that *International Living* covers.

And once again, if Tony and Becky enjoy decent returns on their savings of 5% (before inflation), the savings are on the order of $200,000 under either plan when they reach age 86, Becky's average life expectancy. However, as noted earlier, we are not especially concerned about "happy worries" in this book: Our focus is to identify the baseline plan that delivers a dream life sooner rather than later, together with steadily growing financial security over the long term.

Let's drill down a bit deeper into this case to examine the principal weaknesses in Plan B and consider some options to address them. There are two problems compared to Plan A. First, there is no financial cushion at all before age 70. As noted in an earlier case for Gaby, once Becky reaches age 66 and anytime up to age 70 she has an option at any time to not only start her benefits, but to the start them up to six months retroactively. The benefit is based on the level due as of six months ago, and a lump sum is paid for those months followed by monthly payments thereafter.

One option we have not considered in any previous cases—yet one that applies to all the cases we've seen as well as all that follow—is to find a way to generate some income after relocating. The reason we haven't included it is because it is uncertain for most people, unlike Social Security, which is quantifiable and reliable. Yet the reality is that many, if not most, people can find some work.

Recall that Tony and Becky are both working at the time they leave. They are not unemployed; they are just broke. Maybe one of them can perform some work remotely for their former employer. The internet opens up a multitude of options for conducting business worldwide with little or no overhead. Life overseas opens up opportunities for developing travel articles or photographs for sale. While few countries will offer chances to get a local job that could go to a citizen, the expat community opens many avenues for work for those with the skills: tax prep, house (and pet) sitting, teaching in an English language school, teaching English to locals who need tutoring. This is far from an exhaustive list, and many excellent resources exist to provide suggestions for leveraging anyone's particular skills.

For instance, suppose Tony and Becky each find gigs that generate an average of $500 each per month for four years to age 66. Under either plan this adds $48,000 to the savings by age 66, and that's extra money for the nest egg or for spending, depending on how their overall finances perform.

A second consideration we need to evaluate is what happens in the event of an unexpectedly early death of either spouse. This gets a bit convoluted. We don't write the rules; we just try to help with understanding how they affect us. Stay with us…

First, from the start we have Becky wait to claim at 70 instead of Tony, because all else being equal, she is more likely to live longer and their benefits are equal. (If the benefits were substantially different, the one with the highest benefit claims later to maximize the survivor benefit.) If Becky's health is iffy, Tony should wait to claim instead.

In our example in which Becky waits to claim, if Tony passes away before age 70, Becky would start a survivor claim that would depend on Becky's age when Tony dies. If she is under 66 it will be reduced for early claiming, and if over 66 it will be 82.5% of Tony's FRA benefit of $2,000 (it's reduced because he claimed his benefit early).

That's actually the simple case. What if Becky passes away early? If Tony is under age 66 (recall that Becky is the same age as Tony in this case) he should continue to collect his work-based benefit of $1,500. Then at age 66 he can switch to the survivor benefit, which will equal what Becky would be entitled to at her FRA. If Becky is over 66, Tony will switch to the survivor benefit, which will equal the amount that Becky would have been entitled to receive at the age of her death. For instance, if she passed away at age 68, her FRA benefit of $2,000 would be increased 16% for two years of deferred retirement credits at 8% per year to $2,320.

Got all that? Perhaps we all feel a bit dizzy-headed at this point. As we wrote earlier, when a survivor situation occurs it is probably worth getting some professional advice on how best to proceed.

Key Takeaways

Many folks invested in their lives and their children and then got effectively wiped out during the Great Recession. We can forge a great life overseas on our Social Security benefits alone. Married couples have a great advantage in this regard because they can claim one benefit to live on now while the other one grows and grows. At age 70 they can usually upgrade to a more generous spending budget and still start to save for a rainy day. That sure beats trying to rebuild a nest egg from scratch in our early 60s by grinding it out at the old job. Unless we love that old job, let's pull the ripcord and jump—there's a good chance we will actually end up better off in the long run.

CHAPTER 18
Sarah: Severe Claiming Pitfalls for Survivors
Sarah Must be Cautious When she Becomes Eligible for Survivor Benefits

Sarah and Stuart had long planned to retire to Belize starting in their early 60s. Sadly, as their time to move approached, Stuart fell gravely ill. Medical bills forced them to exhaust much of their retirement savings until Stuart passed away at age 59; Sarah is 62.

Stuart hoped that Sarah would realize their dream retirement, even if he were not along to share it with her. With that in mind, Sarah set out to make their intended move as soon as possible.

Stuart had a $100,000 life insurance policy that helped somewhat to replenish their depleted savings; in addition, $50,000 remained in their retirement accounts. Sarah knows the spending budget that will let her live comfortably: $2,000 monthly throughout her retirement (as always, adjusted for inflation). The question she has is how best to claim her benefits. She sat down with the information shown in the table below to figure out her options.

Case 5: Sarah Moves at 62				
Current Age:		62		
Social Security Benefit At Age:	60	62	66	70
Benefit Monthly – Work	$0	$1,500	$2,000	$2,640
Benefit Annually – Work	$0	$18,000	$24,000	$31,680
Social Security Survivor Benefit				
Benefit Monthly – Survivor	$1,144	$1,296	$1,600	$1,600
Benefit Annually – Survivor	$13,728	$15,550	$19,200	$19,200
Monthly Spending Budget: All-In		$2,000		$2,000
Annual Spending Budget: All-In		$24,000		$24,000
Relocation Spending		$10,000		
Retirement Account Savings		$ 50,000		
Regular Savings (Life Insurance)		$100,000		
Home Sale Net Proceeds		$ 0		
Total Savings Available		$150,000		

Because Stuart passed away right when Sarah turned 62, she is eligible to collect either her work-based benefit or a survivor benefit. Sarah has heard she can collect a survivor's benefit and calls the Social Security Administration to find out how much. She is informed that her survivor benefit will be based on what Stuart would have been eligible to receive at age 66, $1,600. If Sarah claims this amount at age 62, it is reduced for early claiming to $1,296. The SSA agent helpfully points out that Sarah's work-based benefit at 62 would be higher: $1,500 is $204 more per month ($2,448 more per year). She can later apply for the unreduced survivor benefit of $1,600 when she turns 66. That's Plan A. That all seems to make sense: Take the higher benefit now and then switch later to the other one when it is maximized.

As we will see, Sarah is far better off in Plan B, taking the lower survivor benefit now ($1,296) and waiting to switch to her maximized work-based benefit ($2,640) at age 70: give up that extra $204 a month now in order to collect $1,344 more per month at age 70. That's a no-brainer once you look at the numbers, clearly reflected in the cumulative savings comparison below.

Sarah's Savings at Key Age Milestones					
Sarah at Age:	62	70	72	86	91
Plan A: Social Security at 62; Switch to Survivor at 66					
Retirement Account Savings	$ 50,000	$18,000	$10,800	$ 0	$ 0
Regular Savings*	$100,000	$78,800	$76,400	$20,000	$ 0
Total Savings	$150,000	$96,800	$87,200	$20,000	$ 0
Plan B: Survivor Benefit at 62; Switch to Social Security at 70					
Retirement Account Savings	$ 50,000	$ 2,000	$ 1,900	$ 900	$ 600
Regular Savings*	$100,000	$70,400	$85,900	$194,400	$233,100
Total Savings	$150,000	$72,400	$87,800	$195,300	$233,700

*Proceeds from Stuart's life insurance policy.

Sarah's savings under Plan B have already exceeded those under Plan A when she turns 72. By age 86, her average life expectancy, she has nearly 10 times as much in savings—over $175,000 more! Moreover, under Plan A she is collecting $1,600 per month at age 70 (actually since age 66). Under Plan B she is collecting $2,640 beginning at age 70. That's $12,480 more each year.

Plan A shows Sarah running out of savings by the time she reaches age 91; thereafter she will have to live on $1,600 per month. Under Plan B Sarah has a growing stash of savings, and she might even choose to spend more each month. She has no shortage of options.

The difference between these alternatives is displayed starkly in the side-by-side comparison:

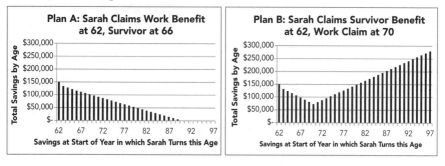

But wait, it could get worse than Plan A. How? When Sarah first applies for benefits it's possible the SSA agent will register her for having applied for both her work-based and her survivor benefit. She is eligible for both at that time. If that happens it would prevent Sarah from switching later to her survivor benefit at age 66 (or vice versa if she applies for survivor benefits first and the amount is higher than her work-based benefit, possible if Stuart's benefit had been high enough). Sarah is unlikely to understand the nuances of restricting her application to only one of the two benefits at 62. This could easily pass her by without her being made aware of valuable future claiming rights that she is giving up in the process. There is some indication that this sort of mistake is not unusual.[77] Yet once it is done, if it isn't recognized and changed in the first year (the "do-over" period), there is every indication that the SSA will not correct it later. The result would be a claiming plan that in Sarah's case would cost her over $200,000 if she lives only to her average life expectancy. That's a lot of money out of her pocket for a clerical error.

Note that in the Case 5 table at the start of this chapter there is a survivor benefit amount indicated for Sarah for age 60. Suppose she is that age when Stuart passes away. While she is too young to collect any work-based benefits from Social Security, she is eligible to collect this survivor benefit of $1,144 a month beginning at that age. (Bear in mind that if

---

she continues to work, the survivor benefit is subject to the same earnings test limits as other benefits if she claims before FRA.) Sarah could start this benefit, make her move, live on $2,000 spending per month, and switch to her maximized work-based benefit at age 70. Between 60 and 70 she can easily make up the difference between this survivor benefit and spending from her savings.

Finally, all the scenarios we have considered here apply equally to Sarah if she is divorced from Stuart and she was married to him at least 10 years. Furthermore, whether married or divorced to Stuart at the time of his death, Sarah cannot have remarried before age 60 or she forfeits any survivor rights on Stuart's work record.

In sum, the survivor rules are among the most complex of all the Social Security benefit claiming situations, especially when the survivor is between 60 and 70 at the time of the death. If such a tragedy happens, we must not let it be compounded by making any claiming decision before we are clearly informed about all the options that will become available to us over time. Do not count on the staff at the Social Security Administration in this regard. There is too much that can go wrong. Unless you are sure, get expert advice.

Key Takeaways

The survivor benefit is a double-edged sword: Claimed effectively, it can provide a finance-saving bridge to our maximized benefit at age 70. However, claimed incorrectly, the cost can be devastating. Get a consultant's assistance with this one if you become a survivor. Too much is at stake not to.

CHAPTER 19
Review, Conclusion, and Getting Started

Whether we are single, married, divorced, or widowed, Social Security has a program for us that will at once confound us with its inexcusable complexity, yet often offer the foundation of what we need in order to establish financial security through what may be many long years as we age. Let's see if we can briefly bring together many of the threads we have developed over the course of this book. Then we will go through a simple, first-step financial plan for our retirement.

Social Security Will be There for us: Plan Accordingly

Almost everyone approaches Social Security with a combination of general uncertainty about how our benefits work and unsubstantiated fears caused by rumors and innuendo that the program is running out of money. As a result, the vast majority claims their benefits early—too early to get the most out of the program. We should know now that it is a far better bet to assume our benefits will be there for us in full and act accordingly.

Most of us Will be Better off by far if we Claim Later

If we live to our average life expectancies once we reach age 62, then we are typically many tens of thousands of dollars ahead if we wait to claim our work-based benefit at 70 and our spouse-based benefit at FRA (age 66 to 67 depending on our birth year).

For Nearly all of us, our Benefits are our Most Valuable Financial Asset

Our benefits are typically worth between $250,000 and $750,000-plus; for a couple that's $500,000 to $1,500,000-plus. That is, it would take that much money in an after-tax savings account to pay an insurance company in order to receive an amount equal to our benefits adjusted each year for inflation. That's much more money than most of us have in our retirement accounts and other savings, as well as more than most of us have as equity in our homes. Like any asset, we have to manage it wisely in order to get the most out of it. For Social Security, that usually means learning what benefit amounts we can receive at various ages, then developing a plan for when to start those benefits.

The good news is that once we have that plan, Social Security is pretty much set-it-and-forget-it after that. No need to meet with the financial advisor (whom we pay one way or the other…) regularly or rebalance a portfolio; no need to mow the lawn all summer and crawl up on the roof each fall to remove the leaves from the gutters and otherwise maintain our homes. We just watch the amount appear in our accounts each month, adjusted yearly for inflation. Done.

Social Security Rules

We summarized these in the "Summary Guide for Determining Your Claiming Options" at the back half of Chapter 11. Beyond reiterating that the rules are complicated, we can't further reduce those points here in any useful way. When in doubt at a critical Social Security claiming juncture, get advice from an independent consultant who specializes in Social Security. It shouldn't cost much, compared with the amount of potential money at stake.

Getting Started: Can we Afford it?

Maybe the cases covered in the last few chapters seem a bit too tidy. We think, "OK, that all makes sense. But where do I start, given my situation?"

If your situation is that you already have more money than you can count, bravo to you—you are already in "happy worry" land! And you probably don't need the following exercise. You just want to follow the instructions elsewhere in this book on getting the most out of the Social Security benefits for which you are eligible. Nothing wrong with adding to your happy worries.

For everyone else—and let's face it, that's most of us—the following blueprint for a starter budget is designed for you.

So here's a starter plan, oversimplified though it may be… We can always complicate it later. (In fact, we provide a guide in Appendix A to help you identify various spending and income items that you can include later in a more detailed budget plan.) For now though, to get you started quickly, simply follow these instructions and you may be on your way to a new life sooner than you imagine:

1. **Establish Age-70 Baseline Guaranteed Income:** If you haven't already, go online and determine the current estimate of your age-70 Social Security benefit amount(s) (see Chapter 11 for detailed instructions). If married and one of you will receive most from a spouse claim, it equals 50% of the worker spouse's FRA benefit, also available online. (The spouse claim should be collected no later than the non-working spouse's FRA—66 or 67 depending on the birth year. While the amount won't go up after that age, it will be reduced if claimed before FRA.) This will establish the baseline of potential spending for the rest of our lives after age 70. Then the question is "How do we make it to age 70 (or FRA for a spouse claim)?"

2. **Identify the Other Financial Resources Available now or in the Future:** We've discussed the biggies here: retirement and regular savings accounts and net proceeds (or loss) from sale of a home. Other sources include anything you might convert to cash: for instance, sale of your business, an anticipated inheritance, and/or net proceeds from a second home. Don't obsess about getting exact numbers. Once you have your starter plan you can go back to fine-tune and update it as you get better information.

3. **Identify any Recurring Sources of Income Besides Social Security:** These might include income from a pension, an annuity, or a trust. Note when these cash streams start: now or at some date in the future.

4. **Identify any Irregular Future Expenses:** You have college expenses for children. You expect to pay for a wedding. Expenditures like those. Guesstimate an amount.

5. **Estimate a Relocation Allowance:** This can include visits to countries where you might like to relocate, travel to your final destination, resident visa costs, any shipping of personal goods, and enough to get established in your new residence. In addition to deposits for a rental home, this can also include furniture, household goods, and starter supplies you may need to purchase locally. Untold thousands of *International Living* readers have kicked off their relocation research by attending one of many cost-effective conferences hosted by *IL* each year in numerous locations in the U.S. and in those countries that are high on the list of expats. Check the back of the magazine or your email inbox for upcoming events.

6. **Emergency Allowance:** How much savings do you want to set aside for this purpose, at least until you reach age 70, when the collection of Social Security benefits permits you to add back to savings if and as needed?

Calculate a Simple Budget Plan: You can do this. This is not rocket science. (We'll do an example in a moment...)

a. Add up all savings sources (#2 above): $ _____

b. Add up lump-sum expenses:

    i. Irregular exp. (#4) $ _____

    ii. Relocation (#5) $ _____

    iii. Emergency (#6) $ _____

    iv. Enter the total of i., ii., and iii. above:

        $ _____

c. Subtract Line b. iv. from Line a.: $ _____

d. Subtract your current age (youngest if married) from 70: _____

e. Divide Line c. by Line d.: $ _____

f. Divide Line e. by 12: $ _____

The number in Line e. is the first rough estimate of the amount available to spend each year between now (your current age) and age 70; Line f. is that same spending amount per month. This is spending available after setting aside money for your contingencies from Line b. iv. (If you have recurring income from #3 above, you can add it to the monthly amount as of the year in which it becomes available.)

Here's a concrete example to better understand this super-simple budget blueprint. Loren and Will are both 61. Their age-70 Social Security benefits (each has a work record) are $2,500 and $1,900, respectively. They have $190,000 in retirement and savings accounts and conservatively estimate they can net $55,000 on the sale of their home. They estimate their relocation budget at $15,000 and are comfortable with a $25,000 emergency fund, since they know their age-70 benefits should allow them to rebuild their savings at that time. Here's their Budget Plan filled in:

7. **Calculate a Simple Budget Plan:**

    a. Add up all savings sources from #2 above: $245,000

    b. Add up lump-sum expenses:

        i. Irregular exp. (#4) $0

        ii. Relocation (#5) $15,000

        iii. Emergency (#6) $25,000

        iv. Enter the total of i., ii. and iii. above: $40,000

    c. Subtract Line b. iv. from Line a.: $205,000

    d. Subtract your current age (youngest if married) from 70:   9

    e. Divide Line c. by Line d.: $22,778

    f. Divide Line e. by 12: $1,898

Now Loren and Will can look into places where they can live well on around $1,900 a month all-in. There are plenty of places around the world where this will take them a long way. It sure beats working and wintering a few more years if that's what they thought they needed to do, the "prudent" thing to do, as so many advisors, family members and friends will surely tell them…

Assuming they would like to build a nest egg at age 70 when their maximized Social Security benefits kick in, they might opt for a spending budget at that point of around $3,000; this would afford all kinds of options for literally luxurious living. Yet because they will be collecting $4,400 a month from Social Security, they could still save $1,400 a month, $16,800 per year. At age 80 that would add $168,000 to their $25,000 in savings for a total of $193,000; at that rate, by 86 (Loren's average life expectancy) they would have $293,800 (in today's dollars)—that's more than they started with at age 61.

Keep in mind that this is a conservative, yet living budget: "conservative" in that it assumes no real return on any savings at any time in the future and "living" in that they can update it constantly based on recent results. Maybe they enjoy better returns on savings for several years or end up spending less. They can loosen their spending accordingly. Perhaps one or both generate some side income that offsets a bit of spending.

Onto this very simple budget we can begin to layer on greater complexity. Ages may vary, so the start of benefits changes accordingly. A pension may start at a certain age…

Loren and Will have many good choices, and they can consider those by simply modifying the blueprint above. As shown, they can spend around $1,900 a month from now to age 70 while they still have at least $25,000 set aside at all times as an emergency fund.

Want to travel more while still younger? Loren and Will should consider a place to live—for a while at least—that costs only about $1,400 a month to live well. These locations are out there! In abundance! And now they have $6,000 a year to spend on travels.

Or they could wait a year. What would that look like? Only eight years would remain to age 70 instead of nine. Replace the "9" in 7. d. with an "8" and recalculate. Line 7. e. changes to $25,625 per year, and Line 7. f. changes to $2,135 per month. (I would vote to start the adventure sooner on a bit less, but that's me.)

As another alternative, if they are nervous about digging too deeply into their savings as they near 70, they could always take one of their benefits a little earlier. That would be Will's because it is lower, so Loren's still maximizes the survivor benefit. Suppose, for instance, Will takes his benefit at age 66: $1,439 a month x 48 months between 66 and 70 is $69,072. This is essentially added to savings (which otherwise dwindle to around $25,000 under the original plan). That's about $94,000 in remaining savings at all times. Then at age 70 their combined benefit is $3,939. They could still spend $3,000 beginning at that age and save $939. The savings would grow to $249,360 by age 86, Loren's average life expectancy.

That's a bit less than the $293,800 they're projected to save under the original blueprint at that age. However, Loren and Will may conclude that it is worth it in order to have more emergency savings in their late 60s. Again, it is a choice with trade-offs that they can simply quantify in this way in order to help them with their decision. All from a super-simple blueprint.

At this point we have our hands firmly on the handful of levers and dials that we need: (1) maximize our projected Social Security benefits; (2) spend less or more; (3) save less or more; and (4) start the adventure sooner rather than later. Work through variations of this budget blueprint to find the setting that feels right to you. May it lead to a formula that gets you to your dream life with long-term financial security sooner rather than later.

Bon voyage!

Key Takeaways

Did you skip to the "Key Takeaways" before reading this chapter? You missed the most valuable advice we have to offer in this book in the form of a simple tool: a step-by-step guide to calculating how much you can have available to spend up to age 70 and thereafter, based on your benefits forecast and savings. Work this through a few times, varying the start year and the spending budgets, and you will soon see that this simple tool can be your key to getting to your dream sooner rather than later.

Summary: Use the tool ➜ Determine a spending budget up to age 70 ➜ Read your *International Living* magazine to find options for where your budget will let you live ➜ Arrange an exploratory visit ➜ Go!

What are you waiting for?

APPENDICES

APPENDIX A
Identifying the Key Pieces of Your Financial Puzzle

The first step in creating your long-term budget plan is to identify the principal financial elements that will apply to your future: the pieces of your financial puzzle. The purpose of this document is to provide you with guidance in identifying those pieces. This is far from an exhaustive list; hopefully the various examples will trigger thoughts in your mind that will help you recognize and add pieces that may not be specifically listed here.

This list is divided into two general sections: (1) types of spending when you move overseas and (2) sources of funds to pay for your spending. The latter section is subdivided into income/earnings streams and savings.

Over the short term there may be years where you have to dip into overall savings in order to cover your expenses in support of a comfortable lifestyle. This can happen in particular during the years you may be waiting to claim your Social Security benefits (usually I recommend closer to age 70 than not). Over the long term a safe planning principal is to be sure that income/earnings streams are more than enough to pay for all the spending with some left over to continually add to savings—that's the formula for a financially secure retirement.

1. **Types of Spending:** Includes day-to-day costs as well as one-time and irregular expenses

   a. Recurring living expenses: While you won't accurately know what these expenses are until you live in your chosen location for a while, you can use your *International Living* resources (starting with the website *http://internationalliving.com*) to obtain reasonable estimates for these costs. The overall living expense estimates commonly include the following (except healthcare, which is often called out separately):

      i. Housing: This is usually the single biggest monthly expense —unless you purchase a home, in which case it is usually a lump sum expense (unusual to obtain a mortgage in most other countries) followed by smaller recurring expense (property taxes, maintenance, etc.)

         Whether renting or owning, this category should include any utility-type expenses (electricity, gas, water, cable, internet, telephone).

         Your timeline may provide for renting when you first relocate, then purchasing a home at a later time. The obvious advantage of home ownership if you find that "rest-of-our-lives" location is that you eliminate rent thereafter, effectively eliminating the risk that you later get priced out of your ideal home because too many others come to discover that your location is extremely desirable as well, driving up rental rates.

      ii. Food: Includes everything you would be consuming at home for meals.

      iii. Entertainment: Restaurants, movies, theater, sports and similar events.

iv. Local Travel:

1. If you own a vehicle: gas, insurance, repairs

2. Public transportation: buses and taxis

v. Items often outside the typical overseas location budgets reported by *International Living*:

1. Healthcare: This is a complicated topic where the best choices depend on your age and health concerns, the country, availability of insurance plans, and so on. Fortunately, healthcare is far more affordable almost anywhere overseas than in the U.S.

2. Taxes: If you are likely to owe them, you better plan for them. The good news is that most people who have Social Security and modest to moderate earnings from investments and savings are unlikely to owe much if anything in income taxes. That's because Social Security benefits are subject to preferable tax treatment that results in little or no tax due if you don't have much in other taxable income.

3. Recurring home country costs: These include storage facilities for items that you don't either liquidate or take with you when you move. Another cost to consider is a mail-forwarding service if you want the convenience of maintaining a local address in the country you are moving away from.

b. Non-Recurring Living Expenses: These include one-off expenses like the purchase of a home. The purpose of the following brief list is to provide some ideas that hopefully trigger a reminder to you of an expense you are aware of but might not have thought of yet.

i. Relocation: Includes at a minimum the flight to your new location, any excess baggage or shipping, and procurement of visas when you make your move. Pre-relocation scouting trips can be added in. To the extent you don't ship many belongings, you may need to allow for local purchases. While many rentals can be found fully furnished and stocked with the basics for a household, others may not. You likely will need property deposits for rentals as well.

ii. Non-Local Travel: This includes any trips back home (and/or trips you may pay to bring family out to visit) as well as other travel in the region or elsewhere in the world.

iii. Wedding(s): Will you be paying for (or contributing to) a family member's wedding at some point down the road?

iv. Education: You may be paying now or in the future for someone's college or other education

v. An around-the-world cruise on your bucket list

Again, this brief list is far from exhaustive and is intended to help you think of any special financial items that could have significant impact for you.

2. **Sources of Funds to Pay for Spending:** For the prior section on "Spending" the quick and easy approach was to use the guidance provided by *International Living* which you can find here: *http://internationalliving.com*. For this next section you need to look to your own set of circumstances to identify the needed information.

   a. **Earnings and Other Income:**

      i. Earnings from work: Perhaps you have an internet-based business you can continue after you move, or you may start a business in your new location; this could be a simple as offering tutoring in English or as complicated as opening a B&B or restaurant.

      ii. Social Security benefits: The key decision point is when to start between ages 62 and 70 for retirement benefits. As you should know by now, this is a complex decision. That said, here's a high level guidance. For singles, try to find a way to make it until 70 unless you either have an extremely short life expectancy or you are financially destitute. For couples, also try to make it to 70. The first compromise on this strategy should be to take the lower potential benefit earlier; the person eligible for the highest benefit should always try to make it to 70 in order to maximize the survivor benefit.

iii. Voluntary and required (RMD) withdrawals from Tax-deferred Savings accounts. These are reportable as taxable income in the year in which withdrawn from these accounts.

iv. Pensions: These vary so much that it is impossible to generalize about them here. If you are eligible for one, this is a good time to look into the terms (when it starts and the monthly payment amount). Keep in mind that many pensions do not adjust for inflation like Social Security benefits do. This means that the amount you start with decreases in purchasing power steadily over time with inflation, in which case it will be less valuable to you as you age.

v. Regular income from investments such as property rentals: For instance, you might own a home and choose to rent it out instead of selling it after you relocate overseas. Consider only the net income (or loss) after all anticipated transaction costs.

vi. Earnings from investment interest or dividends: In the workshop we make the assumption that these earnings are zero after inflation. That's a conservative approach. You will probably do better than that and you can always use any such "excess" earnings down the road to justify an increase in your spending budget.

    vii. One-off and irregular gains (or losses):

        1. Gain (or loss—which would effectively be "negative" income or earnings) on the sale of a property or business (after costs to prepare for sale, agent commissions, tax on any net gain, etc.)

        2. Anticipated inheritance

        3. Other: you may have any number of other potential hard assets (art, antiques, classic car, etc.) that might be converted to savings

    viii. Any other income streams you may have: income from a trust, royalties, and so on.

b. **Regular Savings:** I recommend that you set up your budget plan to use "Regular Savings" as the active line item for settling up your gains and losses at the end of the year somewhat as follows:

    i.   Start the first budget of the first year in your plan with your "Beginning Savings Balance."

    ii. Calculate the difference between your total income (item 2-a, above) and your total spending (item 1, above). If it is positive (i.e., you spend less than all your earnings and other income), then add this to the Beginning Savings Balance to get the End Savings Balance (which is the Beginning Savings Balance for the next year). If the difference is negative (i.e., you spend more than all your earnings and other income for the year), then subtract this from the savings to get the end savings.

c. **Tax-Deferred Savings (IRAs, 401k's, etc.):** Track these savings separately from Regular Savings. Any earnings that occur within such accounts are not taxable until withdrawn, so they stay in these accounts.

    i.   Start with the beginning balance.

ii.   Add any earnings, since these are not taxable until withdrawn.

iii.   Subtract any voluntary withdrawals.

iv.   Subtract any RMD's (Required Minimum Distributions required beginning at age 70.5).

v.   The result is an end balance for tax-deferred accounts that becomes the beginning balance for the next year.

What have we missed? This list is far from exhaustive and meant to get you thinking about the other important financial pieces that apply to your life. Just because it isn't called out in the foregoing doesn't mean that it won't be an important puzzle piece for you.

APPENDIX B
International Living Resources

The author of this book, Steve Garfink is founder of **Social Security Now or Later** (*www.ssnol.com*), a personal and family budgeting service focused on assisting those planning to retire overseas. You determine where, when and how you want to live overseas. Steve works with you to create a plan to ensure your financial security throughout your retirement based on the income sources you have available and the likely expenses you will encounter wherever you relocate.

He is uniquely qualified to provide this service based on his background in budgeting and finance, his expertise on Social Security claiming strategy for those looking to live overseas, and his personal experience that will relocate him along with his wife to Mexico this year. Steve is committed to delivering you an overseas retirement free of financial worry through the rest of your years—may they be many! See Steve's website here: *www.ssnol.com*.

Supplement Your Retirement Overseas with a Fun, Portable Career

These days, the world is more interconnected than ever and the possibilities for a portable paycheck are almost never-ending. You don't need an MBA or thousands upon thousands of start-up cash to create a business for yourself that can easily fund your life overseas.

These are income-generating careers that let you live anywhere in the world, travel any place you please, and create for yourself the quality of life you really deserve. And, when you add your Social Security to the extra income you could receive with a new portable career, you can have the life you've always dreamed of.

Here are some resources to help you get started.

Fund Your Life Overseas

If you'd like to learn more about flexible, work-anywhere ways you can pay for your life overseas, sign up for **Fund Your Life Overseas**, a free e-letter from *International Living*. You'll hear from us five times a week, telling you about ways to earn income that allows you to live anywhere, travel anytime…and give you the funds to make your overseas dream real. Sign up here: *http://internationalliving.com/fund-your-life/*.

International Living's Incomes Abroad

If you—like so many folks—muse about the day you can leave the stress of the rat race behind, grab control of your life, and head off on an adventure abroad… with an income that went with you… That day could be a lot sooner than you think.

Discover and explore the ways you can fund your life overseas and gain the freedom and flexibility of an income that you control with *International Living's* ***Incomes Abroad***. Find out more here: *https://www.ilbookstore.com/In.html*.

21 Days to Your Freelancing Success Abroad

Are you ready to have control over your time, your income, your life? Are you ready to stop answering to a boss and, instead, decide when you'll take vacation…where you'll live…how much you'll make? Then a freelancer's lifestyle could suit you well.

Winton Churchill is behind a special program that shows you how you can use your existing skills to tap into global markets and make money from anywhere in the world. For more details, see *https://www. ilbookstore.com/21-Days-to-Your-Freelancing-Success-Abroad.html.*

The Ultimate Travel Writer's Program

Like the idea of being a travel writer but not sure how to get started? *The Ultimate Travel Writer's Program* can help. With this great course, you can learn the simple secrets and techniques, be writing marketable stories…getting your own by-line…and taking advantage of travel perks…in no time at all. As a freelance writer, you have the opportunity to visit the world's most romantic, exciting, and offbeat destinations. This program has been put together for people interested in taking up the travel writer life. For more information, see: *https://www.ilbookstore.com/ The-Ultimate-Travel-Writer-s-Program-Online-Program.html.*

AWAI's Accelerated Program for Six Figure Copywriting

Imagine…you can live anywhere…Prague…Costa Rica…the Portugal Coast… You can work when you want, choose your boss, make a six-figure income, and get paid in American dollars… What can be better than that? Find out how to get started, here: *https://www.ilbookstore.com/AWAI-s-Accelerated-Program-for-Six-Figure-Copywriting.html.*